God,
the
Mafia,
My Dad,
and Me

God,
the
Mafia,
My Dad,
and Me

A True Story of Secrets *and* Survival

Lori Lee Peters

LIONCREST
PUBLISHING

GOD, THE MAFIA, MY DAD, AND ME
A True Story of Secrets and Survival

ISBN   978-1-5445-2594-5   *Hardcover*

        978-1-5445-2592-1   *Paperback*

        978-1-5445-2593-8   *Ebook*

For my Dad, my mentor, my hero. You saved me with your love, presence, passion, and undeniably unique brand of humor.

For my inner child, may you now have peace.

Contents

Prologue

It has been a week since I learned I will be killed.

I'm lying in bed, unable to sleep, desperately trying to come up with a plan to stay alive. I don't know when my killer will appear, but when he does, there will be nowhere to hide.

My killer has every advantage. He is scary smart, afraid of no one and nothing. When he inevitably acts, he will suffer no consequences. I could kill myself before he finds me, but I won't give him the satisfaction. Besides, I don't want to die. I'm only thirteen years old.

As I lie in bed, I go over my options again and again, but I realize I have none. I can't tell a soul what I've learned because I'm too afraid to talk about it. I'm shaking uncontrollably, even though I have the blankets pulled up to my chin. Finally, I can't take it anymore.

"Dad! Dad!" I yell.

Seconds later, my mom rushes in. "What's wrong, Lori?" she asks.

"No, Mom," I say through my tears. "I need Dad."

If anyone can protect me, it's my dad, my superhero.

Mom leaves, and a couple minutes later, my dad walks in. Before he reaches my bed, I blurt out, "Dad, I can't stop shaking."

"What's the matter, honey?" he asks as he sits on the bed next to me and takes my hand.

"I'm scared."

"Why are you so scared?"

I pause, then shake my head and say, "I can't tell you."

"You know you can tell me anything."

"I really want to, Dad. I wish I could, but I just can't. I'm too afraid. Dad, please stay with me until I fall asleep."

"I'll stay right here," he says as he lies down on his back next to me. "Try to stop shaking, honey."

Not telling my dad what's wrong is the most gut-wrenching decision I have ever made, but I know with every fiber of my being that if I tell him, that will be the end of me. If Dad, my hero, says it's true that I will die, I will erupt into a million pieces.

Despite my terror, I can't take that chance.

I feel so safe with my dad lying next to me. Eventually, I stop shaking and drift off to sleep, hoping his presence will be enough to shield me from my enemy, from the killer who lies in wait.

After all, God is my killer.

My Dad

L ouis Edward Peters was born in New York City on August 9, 1931, in the midst of the Great Depression. The family struggled to find enough food, and my dad's mother frequently stood in the soup line while nursing her infant son. After several difficult years, Dad was sent to live with his grandparents and two uncles in Carmel, Maine, where his father felt he would be better cared for.

At four years old, Dad struggled to adjust to his new life on a farm in the middle of nowhere with people he had never met. He clung to his teddy bear and carried it everywhere, wondering when he would see his parents again.

At age six, Dad started grammar school in Damascus, Maine, about a half-mile from the farm in Carmel. On the first day, Dad discovered that he was the only child in his grade. In total, twelve students in Kindergarten through eighth grade attended the one-room schoolhouse.

To the kids from Maine, someone from New York was a foreigner, so my dad stood out from the beginning. Then the other students discovered Dad's father came from Greece, and the real teasing started. During the first couple of weeks, the older kids called Dad "greaseball," which led to yelling matches but never ended in a fistfight.

Over the next few years, Dad made friends in Carmel, and together they played basketball and slid down snow-covered hills. During the summer, they camped out under the stars and talked about what they wanted to become.

Summers also involved fishing with his grandfather. They would go to the general store—which had everything from groceries to hardware—to pick up a bamboo pole and some line so they could fish for pickerel and white perch among the frogs and lily pads.

The one-room schoolhouse gave Dad more than a good education. Through the daily practice of reciting the morning prayer and standing for the Pledge of Allegiance, Dad gained a respect for God and country—a country where a little farm boy from Maine could grow up and become anyone and anything he wanted.

After sixth grade, Dad attended a brand-new multi-room school that covered seventh through twelfth grade. In December of his seventh-grade year, he jumped to the eighth grade and graduated second in his class of eleven. During his freshman year, however, Dad had a disagreement with the principal that couldn't be resolved. As a result, Dad quit high school after the ninth grade and started working on his grandparents' farm. During the summer, he plowed the fields with a team of horses and planted beans, corn, potatoes, and strawberries. During the harsh Maine winters, he and his horses hauled cut lumber from the woods to trucks headed to the sawmill.

For the first seven years that Dad lived on the farm, his parents rarely visited. Then, when my dad was eleven, his father had a heart attack and spent a few weeks in the veterans hospital in Maine. When he was released, my grandfather returned to New York City and to his job as a baker, while my expecting grandmother stayed on the farm with her parents, her brothers, and my dad. There, she gave birth to Paul, my dad's younger brother. My grandfather was again hospitalized in Maine when my dad was sixteen. This time, when he was released, he stayed on the farm with his wife and children. For the first time since he was four, my dad lived under the same roof as his father and could finally get to know him.

During that time together, my grandfather passed on his baking skills, which helped my dad find work at a bakery in Bangor, Maine, as well as one in Waterville, to help support the family. He also began selling portrait appointments for Olan Mills Studios.

One night when he was eighteen, my dad ran out of gas while driving back to the farm after work. He was in a rural area without a gas station for miles around, so he walked to a nearby car and siphoned two gallons out of the tank, just enough to get back home. Unfortunately, as he screwed the tank cap back on, a policeman drove around the corner and caught him in the act. Dad spent the night in jail, and the next morning in court, the judge fined him fifty dollars and gave him six months' probation.

That event changed my dad's life. He recognized his mistake and vowed to never put himself in that position again. He wanted to make something of his life, something beyond working in bakeries and selling portraits.

Dad also wanted to make amends for his actions, so in December 1950, after he finished probation, Dad joined the Marine Corps and was shipped off to Paris Island, South Carolina, for boot camp, where he proved to be a sharpshooter with an M1 Garand rifle, winning the silver badge by scoring 212 out of a possible 250. After basic training, Dad spent a month at Camp Pendleton in California, and then left for Korea aboard the *USS Pope*, which carried nine thousand troops with the ninth draft.

Dad's unit arrived behind the line in the evening. The commanding officer instructed his unit to dig foxholes, but between the frozen ground and exhaustion, they only dug three to six inches deep. When Dad and his unit awoke to mortar rounds all around them at two in the morning, they quickly got up and started digging deeper.

Later that morning, while the unit walked to the line, Dad wondered if he could actually shoot another human being. When he arrived at the front and saw all the wounded and dead Marines, however, something in him changed, and he didn't have a problem after that. Seeing those soldiers on the ground made a man out of him very quickly. When it came time to fight, he fought. When it came time to shoot, he shot. One time when engaged in hand-to-hand combat, he was struck by a bayonet. He didn't lie down and cry; he kept fighting because he knew if he didn't, the enemy would kill him.

A few months later, a major from Washington DC visited Korea to teach Dad's unit the latest techniques in hand-to-hand combat. According to my father, the major wore dress khakis and looked like he walked straight out of *GQ Magazine*.

Because my dad was a big guy like the major, he was picked to be part of the demonstration. The major told Dad to run over the knoll and come straight at him with his M1. It wasn't every day that a sergeant had a chance to face off against a major, and Dad didn't want to be insubordinate, so he carried his rifle more loosely than he normally would. As a result, the major knocked the M1 out of Dad's hand and hit him in the balls so hard he almost passed out.

"Did you have to do that?" my dad asked, gasping.

The major laughed. "You weren't protecting yourself very well. Come at me again."

As soon as he caught his breath, Dad ran back over the ridge. If the major thought the guys on the line were a bunch of pansies, Dad would show him otherwise; he was already battling every day, so if the major wanted a fight, Dad was more than willing to oblige. This time when he approached the major, Dad held his rifle tightly. When the major tried the same move, my dad used his M1 to knock the gun out of his hand and then swung his M1 back and hit him across the face, breaking his jaw and knocking out half his teeth. That was the end of the major's trip to Korea. He was immediately taken to the medical station and then sent back to the States. Dad was concerned that he might be court-martialed, but that never came to pass.

During his time in Korea, Dad became a sergeant with the First Marine Reconnaissance Division in the area around Heartbreak Ridge, including Punchbowl. He also participated in the first mass troop landing in a helicopter. One day when my dad's unit returned from a training exercise, he learned that there was an advancement notice for Marine Corps sergeants and that his colonel had recommended him. The only problem was that the Marines required a high school diploma for this promotion, and my dad hadn't gone past the ninth grade. The colonel told Dad to go to special services, where he could take a four-hour high school equivalency exam. If he passed, he would meet the requirement and be on his way to Quantico, Virginia, to become a lieutenant. Dad passed the exam, but the results came back three days after training in Quantico started, and he lost his opportunity to advance.

On December 3, 1953, he was honorably discharged from the Marine Corps and returned to Maine and to his job as a door-to-door salesman for Olan Mills Studios. But that only lasted for a couple of weeks. Dad knew he didn't want to sell door to door for the rest of his life and that he needed an education to move ahead, so he decided to study engineering at the University of Maine. When he applied for the winter semester, the man at the admissions desk asked about his high school grades.

"I didn't finish high school, but I passed the equivalency test," Dad told him.

"Well, there is no way you can attend the University of Maine. You haven't even been to school. You need to go to prep school and take these courses...then come back."

"I don't have that kind of time," my dad replied. "What if I become a physical education instructor instead?"

The man shook his head. "There is no way you can get into the University of Maine. You are not qualified and could never pass."

With that, my dad turned around and walked out. Within a week, he applied to Husson College, a small private school with about five hundred students. Dad met with Mr. Husson himself on three separate occasions, and he was accepted on a trial basis, using his high school equivalency exam.

Dad jumped around to different majors but finally decided on accounting. In 1957, he graduated with a finance degree and a 3.8 grade point average. From there, he was accepted into Michigan State University master's program in finance.

With his acceptance letter in hand, my dad returned to the University of Maine and found the same man sitting behind the admissions desk.

"I don't know if you remember me," my dad said as he set his acceptance letter on the desk. "But I was here four years ago and wanted to go to the University of Maine. You told me I would never make it. Well, I'm here to tell you that I graduated from Husson College, and I've been accepted at Michigan State University for graduate school. I did make it. You should always give an individual an opportunity to try because you never know what they might be able to do and what you might be turning away."

Dad picked up his acceptance letter, said thank you, and walked out, leaving the man speechless.

* * *

During his first year at Husson, Dad met an attractive freshman named Marilyn, who was in the office management program and grew up in Washburn, Maine. Like my dad, she was the older of two children.

My dad started dating Marilyn soon after they met, and on February 18, 1956, while they were both still students, my parents married. Mom held a job in an army recruiting office for a while and was the secretary for a business management firm, and then worked part time when they started having children. My older sister Leslie was born in Bangor, Maine, in 1957. I was born in 1960 after they moved to Michigan for graduate school, as was my sister Lisa, in 1966.

My parents were, to coin a phrase, a handsome couple. Photos taken at various functions show they were always impeccably dressed: my dad with a fresh haircut, tailored suit, shiny cufflinks, and polished shoes; my mom in a fashionable dress, hair and makeup done to perfection to tastefully highlight her beauty.

* * *

While attending Michigan State University, my dad received job offers from Cadillac Motor Car Division, Ford Motor Company, General Electric, and the state's General Accounting Office; in January 1959, he started working as a clerk at Cadillac.

Throughout college, Dad had held one to two jobs and was accustomed to putting in long hours. After working the 11:00 p.m. to 7:00 a.m. shift as a motel clerk, Dad attended classes from 8:00 a.m. to 4:00 p.m. and then grabbed a few hours of sleep before going back to work. During the summer, he worked as a swim instructor for the city pool in addition to taking the nightshift at the motel.

Dad applied the same work ethic at Cadillac, but after three months, he was called into the office and told that he could no longer work overtime and that if he did work past five o'clock, he would be let go. Dad was stunned. He regularly finished his eight-hour-a-day job in six hours. He asked for more work—and they piled it on—but he was not satisfied with being a clerk. He wanted to work his way up to executive within General Motors.

My dad continued to work past five, telling himself management wouldn't actually follow through with their threat, but management was serious. They gave him an ultimatum, and Dad complied—on his terms. Instead of working late, he started coming in at four or five in the morning so he could work the same number of hours. No one was going to tell him how hard he could work. Dad was stubborn and had a bit of an ego, but he also took great pride in what he did.

Dad later learned that management's ultimatum resulted from a fear that the union might discover Dad was working ten to twelve hours a day, as well as a distrust of gung-ho new hires whose fire eventually burned out and caused problems for the company. A year earlier, one such employee had been working overtime and then sued after an incident occurred during the overtime hours; management didn't want another lawsuit.

In 1967, after eight years of putting in long hours and moving up in the company, his time came for another promotion. At first, Dad thought he was receiving a lateral transfer from Michigan to California, and he approached the executive office about it.

In response, one of the executives asked, "Who is retiring out in San Francisco?"

"Lou Mayor," my dad responded.

"That's right. That's your new job."

"But I'm a level-six employee. Lou Mayor is level eight."

"Yes, you're the first person in the history of Cadillac to receive a double promotion."

Dad was floored, one of the few times he was speechless.

Around the same time, Dad received another unexpected surprise: he was voted one of the most outstanding young men of America in 1967 by the junior chamber of commerce of the Southern United States, and received a plaque recognizing this achievement.

Dad's hard work and persistence had finally paid off in a big way. He was promoted to district sales manager for Cadillac in the San Francisco zone, and my family moved to nearby Cupertino.

Me

We were living in Michigan when I started elementary school at age four. I still remember my first day, dressed in a pastel pink, white, and blue striped dress with white socks and shoes. My blonde hair was pulled back into a ponytail tied with a white ribbon. I raced to the car that morning and bounced in my seat during the twenty-minute ride. Even at that age, I was curious and loved meeting new people, so I just knew Kindergarten was going to be fun. And I was right: my first day, I made a new friend and decided that visiting her house sounded far more interesting than going home, so that's what I did. I'm still not sure how my mom found me.

Within a month or two, my teacher could see my curiosity coming through in my interactions with classmates. On my first report card, she wrote, "Lori can be so slow and poky! She gets interested in others and then takes forever to finish."

Toward the end of the school year, we were given two lists of careers, divided into a boys column and a girls column. The boys side had jobs like *fireman, policeman, cowboy, astronaut, soldier,* and *baseball player,* while the girls side had *mother, nurse, schoolteacher, airline hostess, model,* and *secretary.* The idea was that we would check off careers we liked from the gender-appropriate column, but I picked every career in both columns. They all sounded fascinating, and I wanted to learn more about every single one. I even added a career at the bottom of each list: "sharef" (sheriff) on the boys side and "yard duty" on the girls. My widespread interest wasn't too far from reality: as an older child, I channeled my inner cowboy while riding ponies bareback through open fields, holding onto the mane and loving every minute, and the baseball player came out when I played fastpitch softball for eight years. As an adult, I became a flight attendant for three airlines, dabbled in modeling, and worked as a secretary for my dad. I also tested to become a police officer and made it all the way to the final interview stage.

Other than Kindergarten, my Michigan memories revolve around being outside. While the rest of my family was content to sit inside and read, I wanted to explore nature and the world around me. I often trekked through the backyard in my thick leaf-patterned coat, looking at the trees, leaves, and every creature I could find. I'd also put on my roller skates, the kind you buckled on to your regular shoes, and race down the driveway and sidewalk, thrilled at the breeze in my face and hair.

* * *

I was seven when my dad received the double promotion that took us to Cupertino. That same year, I found our black cat, Misty, lying in the street. I ran home, crying, and as soon as I opened the door, I yelled, "Dad, come quick! Misty is lying in the street at the corner. Dad, come get her. Hurry!"

We lived by a busy street, and I'm sure Dad knew Misty was part of the pavement, but he still got up right away to help me.

"Okay, Lori, I just need to grab a couple things."

"Hurry, Dad!"

Dad brought out a shovel and box, and we walked to the corner. "Dad, there she is!" I yelled as soon as I saw Misty on the busy street near the gutter.

"Lori, I'm going to pick up Misty, but I need your help to direct traffic away from me, okay?" my dad said.

I nodded. "Is she dead, Dad?" I asked.

"Yes, sweetie. I think she is."

I turned around to face the oncoming traffic. Tears streamed down my face as I waved my arms toward the other lane, saying, "Go around. Go around."

I kept sneaking glances back at my dad as he scraped up Misty with the shovel and placed her in the box. When he finished, he said, "Okay, honey. I've got Misty now. You did a great job helping. Let's go home."

I dropped my arms and followed him onto the sidewalk, wiping away tears.

As we walked home, I asked, "What are we going to do with Misty?"

"I think we should bury her in the backyard," Dad replied.

"Won't she be cold?"

"When we get home, you can get one of your doll blankets, and we can put the blanket on top to keep her warm. Do you think Misty would like that?"

"Yes, Dad."

As soon as we reached the house, I ran into my room to choose the perfect blanket. Then Dad and I walked to the backyard. While I covered Misty with the blanket, Dad dug a hole. Then he placed the box inside and covered it with dirt.

When he was done, Dad put away the shovel, and we returned to the house.

Later that day, I found Dad and asked, "Where is Misty now? Where did she go?"

"Well, she's in heaven, honey."

"What's heaven?"

"That's where we go when we die."

"When does that happen?"

Question after question poured out of my heavy heart. Finally, Dad said, "Lori, you don't need to worry about that now. Misty is in heaven, and she's happy. That's all you need to know, sweetheart."

But it wasn't. I wanted, I needed, to know more. This was my first experience with death, and I didn't understand what had happened. I could tell Dad was uncomfortable talking about it, but in my curious seven-year-old mind, his reluctance translated to "Death is a bad thing. Death isn't something you talk about." If heaven was such a good thing, why wasn't he happy to talk about it? Wouldn't you *want* to talk about something fun?

Around four years later, I came home from school to find that my pet rat was gone. Not just my rat, but his cage, too.

"Mom, how come Chip's not in here?" I called from my bedroom.

"Oh, Lori, I'm sorry. Chip died," she replied as she walked in. "I didn't want you to see that, so I took care of it."

"What? I didn't get to say goodbye."

"The cage is out in the garage if you want to go look."

I walked out and stared at the empty cage. I couldn't believe it. Chip was just gone. "I miss you," I said as I started to cry.

Mom followed me out to the garage and asked if I was okay. After I said yes, she returned to the house. I never found out where she put Chip, but I knew not to ask. She clearly didn't want to talk about it.

When my grandfather—my dad's dad—died a few years after Chip, the same shroud of secrecy hung over the situation. My parents took my sisters and me to the funeral at the Greek church, but we didn't go to the cemetery. I never even saw the coffin. I guess my parents thought they were protecting us, but for me, it only intensified this frightening unknown called *death*.

Like puberty, sex, religion, and other uncomfortable subjects, death was simply something we didn't talk about in our family. This was a tough reality for someone with my intense curiosity and thirst for knowledge. Though my dad tried, his evident discomfort, as well as my mom's avoidance, gave me the sense that the world was filled with secrets—things that I wasn't supposed to know or ask about—and this informed my understanding of what I could discuss and what thoughts I simply needed to keep inside.

* * *

My parents didn't show much affection toward each other, at least not in front of my sisters and me. Once I figured out how babies were made, I got it into my head that I must have been adopted. After all, if my parents didn't kiss and hug, then they probably didn't have sex either.

With my sisters and me, Mom was kind and caring but not what I would call affectionate. She hugged us in the polite way she might embrace a friend. She tended to our physical needs, made sure we were clothed and fed, and nursed us when we were sick, but she kept her emotions under control. I never saw her cry until I was an adult, and she rarely laughed out loud, instead smiling and shaking her head as if to say, "You guys."

The only time I saw real joy on Mom's face was when Dad swung her around as they danced the jitterbug. I loved watching them dance. They were light on their feet and moved with precision and grace. It was beautiful, partly because I could tell mom loved that part of my dad and enjoyed their connection as they danced.

Dad was just the opposite. He was gregarious and laughed often, and he lavished us with warm bear hugs. Sometimes when he wrapped us in his arms, he would say, "I love you! I want you to always know how much I love you because I didn't have that from my mom and dad." Mom, on the other hand, said "love you," rather than "I love you," and I always felt the difference.

Mom was also a very private person. On any given morning before school, I might knock on her bedroom door and say, "Can I come in? I want to ask you about…"

Inevitably, the response was a brusque, "No, not now. I'm getting ready. I'll be out in a minute."

Even if I didn't have a specific question, I would have liked to watch Mom's daily routine, partly as a way to connect with her and partly because I was curious about how she put on and took off her makeup and how she did her hair. But she was too private for that. Anything I learned about personal hygiene, makeup, tweezing my eyebrows, and so on, I learned from my sister Les, who probably learned it from her friends.

Dad, on the other hand, had an open-door policy. Anytime I needed to ask him a question, he was available, even if he was in the bathroom shaving.

One time we were in the bathroom, talking. As I watched him shave, I suddenly asked, "Dad, why are black people's teeth so white? They're so pretty."

Without skipping a beat or making me feel like this was an odd question, he said, "Well, Lori, we all have white teeth."

"But their teeth look better. They're *so* white."

Dad put down his razor and took two white combs out of the top drawer and held them next to each other. "Do you see any difference between these combs?" he asked.

"No, they look the same."

"Right," he said and then put down one of the white combs and picked up a black one and held it next to the other white one. "Now do you see a difference? See how the white stands out more?"

"Yeah."

"Well, that's why black people's teeth look whiter. They stand out more against their dark skin."

"Ohhhh. Okay. Thanks, Dad." And then I wandered out of the bathroom and got ready for school.

I tried to form a similar connection with my mom, especially as I got older, but I found it difficult because our personalities were so different. Sometimes if she was looking out the kitchen window while I was outside, I would make a silly face or walk with bent, shaky legs and wobbly arms to see if I could get a reaction. She might smile and shake her head, but she maintained control and never responded with outright laughter.

Many years later, after I had changed careers and moved out of state, my mom said, "You know, you're a lot like your dad." My mom really disliked change, so I'm not sure she meant it as a compliment, but I took it that way. I loved my dad for his openness, sense of humor, unconditional love toward me, and passion for achievement. Though he didn't know it, Dad provided a sense of stability and safety that I desperately needed, especially in the years to come.

* * *

In addition to his position as a district sales manager, Dad owned a laundromat in Cupertino, and I sometimes went with him when he checked in on the weekends. He always engaged customers with a smile on his face. He would ask how they were doing and whether he could get them anything, and he would always introduce me, which made me feel so grown up and special.

One Saturday, Dad brought along some work pants that needed to be washed. When they were done, he gave me some quarters and asked me to put his pants in the dryer on Permanent Press, but he didn't mention the heat setting. When the dryer stopped, I pulled out one pair of pants and held them up. They looked a lot shorter than when I had put them in.

"Uh, Dad, I think something happened to your pants," I said as he walked over.

I handed him the pants, and he held them against his legs and looked down. The ends of the pant legs sat above his ankles. He looked up at me, smiling.

"Well," I said, "they don't look too bad. You could turn them into shorts."

"Or fancy swim trunks!" my dad said, and we both laughed.

"I'm sorry I ruined your pants, Dad."

"No, sweetheart. It was my fault for not telling you what temperature setting to use."

As Dad removed the other pants from the dryer, he said, "Well, it looks like I need to go shopping!"

Our visits to the laundromat included cleaning the washing machines, gathering quarters from the machines that weren't in use, and stacking rolls of quarters into the paper sleeves. As we worked, I peppered Dad with questions.

"Why do we clean the washing machines? Don't they get clean when people wash their clothes?"

"Well, no, they can get dirty around the top and under the lid and in the slot where people put detergent."

"What's that machine?" I asked, pointing toward the wall.

"That's a change machine. You put in a dollar bill, and the machine gives you four quarters that you can use in the machines."

"Why are we putting the quarters in these sleeves? Why can't we just stuff them in a bag?"

"That's the way the bank wants the coins turned in. We have to make sure we put in the exact amount that's written on the sleeve," he said, pointing to the numbers.

"Okay, I'll make sure." I took extra time to make sure each sleeve had the exact amount. I wanted to make Dad proud. I wanted to show him that he could count on me.

As with the questions I posed while my dad shaved, Dad always answered thoughtfully and patiently. He never made me feel weird about my insatiable curiosity. Instead, he fed my desire to know and learn.

Dad also taught me about running a business. He told me how important it was to be friendly and treat people with respect, no matter who they are. He taught me the importance of keeping the laundromat clean so people would enjoy doing business there and want to come back.

"That's why I have this drink machine here," he said. "It takes time to do laundry, and people like to have something to drink."

Much later in life, when I opened my own business, I used these valuable tips and many more.

* * *

One of the best parts of living in Cupertino was our neighborhood. We knew everyone on our street. The kids all played hide and seek and street football, the families held block parties, and the dads got together monthly to play poker.

Sometimes my dad let me hang out while they played cards. He called me his good luck charm. At one of their poker games, my dad left the table, claiming he had to get something from our house. The other guys kept playing. Suddenly, a tall man in a sheriff's uniform, sunglasses, and hat flung open the sliding glass door, and said, "This is a bust!" Everyone immediately dropped their chips, fear in their eyes. Then Dad started laughing and took off his hat and glasses.

"Jesus, Lou. What the hell!" one of the guys said. Then everyone burst out laughing. That was Dad, always looking for a chance to have fun, this time using his volunteer sheriff's uniform.

I didn't understand the game of poker, but I enjoyed being with the men. The moms were always discussing kids and school, and I found the dads' talk about sports and hobbies much more interesting. Plus, I liked their funny stories and the feel of the room—guys getting together to have drinks and play cards.

Our family became especially close with the Elswoods, who lived next door and always had a houseful of people and fun. Bob and Betty had three children: Cathy, the oldest; Robin, who was my sister Leslie's age; and Art, who was two years younger than me and became my best friend. The Elswoods also had a pool, so their house was the hangout spot in the summer.

I was particularly drawn to Betty, who was the opposite of my mom in many ways. While Mom remained reserved and polite, Betty was animated and affectionate, always giving out hugs, always ready for a good chat. While my mom never played games with us or joined us in the pool, Betty had no problem putting on her bathing suit and swimming with us kids. She was the first busty woman I had seen in person, and after seeing her prominent cleavage in her one-piece bathing suit, I thought, *So, this is a woman!*

Around 1967, we went camping as a family for the first time, and Bob and Betty and their kids joined us. When we arrived, my dad unloaded the car and helped us put up the tent and set up camp. We ate dinner, sat around the campfire, and made s'mores. When we were finished, Dad abruptly stood up and said, "Okay. I'll see you guys tomorrow."

My sisters and I all looked at each other. "What are you talking about? Where are you going?" we asked.

Dad made some excuse and said, "I'll be back in the morning. Have fun!" and then he drove off. Something felt off, but Mom went along with the excuse. More secrets.

Years later when we were adults, Dad told us that when stationed in Korea, he slept on the ground every night for months at a time. When he returned, he swore that he would never sleep on the ground again. Ever. True to his word, any time we went camping, my dad drove us to the site, helped us set up, and hung out around the campfire, and then drove to a motel for the night and joined us the next morning.

I loved living in Cupertino. We had wonderful friends and neighbors, and despite my disconnection from Mom, I was a happy kid who enjoyed all the normal kid things: being mommy to my lifelike doll, hanging out with my best friend, swimming on long summer days.

Just a few years later, I would long for those innocent, carefree days.

My Dad

About three years after transferring to the San Francisco zone, Dad checked in on a dealership in Lodi, California, that hadn't been doing well financially. During the call, the owner said, "Lou, find me a buyer. I want to sell."

"I have a buyer," my dad replied.

"Well, who is it?"

"It's me."

Dad had already been considering the possibility of owning a dealership, and this was the perfect opportunity. He bought Tokay Motors in 1970, and our family moved to Lodi that summer.

At first, Dad sensed that people didn't appreciate him taking over this long-established business. Perhaps it was because Lodi was a small town back then, and he was viewed as an outsider. Perhaps it was because many businesses took the name Tokay, after a certain grape used in wine production, and he changed the dealership name to Peters Pontiac-Cadillac-GMC Incorporated. Perhaps it was because he wasn't German like a lot of the residents at that time. Whatever the reason, it didn't matter. Dad was determined to run an honest, successful dealership that treated its customers and employees right.

Dad's hard work paid off from the beginning. When he bought Tokay Motors, the business was on the verge of bankruptcy. The dealership had never made more than $25,000 in any one year. In the first year under Dad's ownership, however, the dealership made $87,000, then $192,000 in the second year. In the first two years, Dad made more money than the former owner had in the previous twenty-three. When the energy crisis hit in 1973, sales dropped off, but soon after, business picked up again.

A couple years after Dad bought the dealership, the local paper started printing a four-page insert called *Peters Progress* in which my dad featured cars for sale or lease, thanked customers for their business, shared news about special events, and explained his business values, such as the dealership's "no pressure tactics." He also highlighted employees from different departments—the body shop, sales, office managers, and so on— including a photo and a short bio.

Dad was a hands-on boss who rewarded hard work, whether through a write-up in the *Peters Progress*, bonuses, gifts, or even trips. He encouraged all employees, regardless of gender, age, or race, to work hard and take advantage of the endless opportunities within General Motors at large, as well as his dealership. But not everyone shared my dad's work ethic. It drove him crazy when salespeople sold a lot of cars Monday through Wednesday and then chose not to come in on Thursday and Friday. Dad was fair, but if people weren't willing to put in the work, he ultimately let them go so he could give others an opportunity to succeed.

My dad was also generous with his employees, and in general. He didn't take people or circumstances for granted. He never forgot the opportunity Mr. Husson had given him. Though Mr. Husson had passed away, Dad still wanted to give back to the school that had educated him and prepared him to be the successful businessman he had become. My dad donated $50,000 toward a new student lounge at Husson College, and in 1972, with Mom at his side, Dad cut the ribbon at the dedication ceremony in his honor.

* * *

Within a year or two of moving to Lodi, my mom decided to have a garage sale. In the days leading up to it, she spent hours gathering and pricing items to sell. My dad sold used cars at his dealership, but he saw those as having real value, unlike our used household items and clothing. He never visited the sales rack at a store, and he simply couldn't fathom why anyone would buy our unwanted, used stuff.

"Nobody is going to come here and buy our crap," he declared.

"People will come," my mom assured him.

The morning of the garage sale, my dad heard noises out front and peeked out the window.

"You've got to be kidding me!" he said. "It's 7:30 in the morning. There are already people here, thirty minutes early!"

When we opened the garage door at eight o'clock, people streamed in, buying things left and right. Dad couldn't believe it. He decided he wanted a piece of the action. He set up a chair in the garage and started wheeling and dealing. Ever the salesman, he bartered and joked with his customers, getting them excited about buying our "crap."

I loved watching Dad in action, completely in his element. His warm, friendly way with people left a deep impression, one that I carried into my own business as an adult. In the end, my dad turned our one and only family garage sale into a successful and memorable event.

* * *

My dad was a big man, way too big for the white bamboo furniture we had in our family room. Whenever he sat down, his knees came up to his chest because his heavy frame sank down *soo* far into the cushion. Even with pieces of plywood under the cushions to prop him up a little, he looked like a giant sitting on dollhouse furniture.

One day he decided he had had enough of that uncomfortable furniture. He wanted to buy himself a leather recliner, "a real man's chair." He borrowed a pickup truck from the dealership and took my sister Leslie, her friend Robin, and me with him to select a new chair.

We browsed around the store for a while, and my dad picked out a beautiful brown leather recliner, big enough for all six-foot-three of him to relax in comfort. Dad brought the truck around to the back of the store, and two men from the store loaded the chair into the bed.

"Do you have any ropes or anything to tie it down?" one of them asked.

"I didn't bring any," my dad replied. "I don't think we'll need them. It's so heavy. It's not going anywhere."

"You know, you should probably tie it down," the other guy said.

"No, no. It'll be fine. We don't have far to go." Dad left out the fact that we would be driving home on Highway 99.

So the guys shut the tailgate, and we headed back to the highway just as darkness fell. As we drove along in the fast lane, my dad said, "Lori, will you look back every now and again, just to make sure everything's okay."

"Sure, Dad," I replied, while thinking, *It's a big truck. What could go wrong?*

My sister and Robin were sitting up front with my dad, and I was sitting in the back seat, so I turned sideways so I could listen to their conversation and frequently check on the chair.

Everything was fine for about ten minutes. Then I looked back, and the chair was gone. *Oh crap!* I thought.

"Uh, Dad," I said nervously. "The chair's not there."

"What do you mean the chair isn't there"?

"It's not there. It's gone."

Dad took a quick glance back, muttered something under his breath, and then pulled over into the narrow median next to the fast lane. He got out and walked back a half-mile or so, then returned to the truck, likely cursing the whole way.

"Did you find the chair? Where is it?" I asked when he got behind the wheel.

"It's in the oleander bushes," he said, referring to the bushes that create a barrier between the north and south sides of the four-lane highway. Thankfully, the chair had landed there and not in one of the lanes.

Dad started the truck and slowly backed up all the way to the recliner sitting in the bushes. Les and Robin got out to help while I watched from the back seat. I'm certain Dad was not happy, but beyond a few words muttered under his breath, he never let it show. After the chair was retrieved and the three of them returned to the front seat, all he said was, "It's fine. We're going to take it home. I'm sure it's going to be just fine."

When we arrived, my sister and Robin helped Dad bring the chair into the house, where we all got a good look at it. The oleander branches had torn the leather in a few places, but otherwise it didn't look too bad. Then Dad hesitantly sat down. When he reclined, the whole chair leaned to the side, so he was lying at an angle. The chair was clearly broken to all of us...except Dad.

"Oh, Dad, the chair is broken." I felt bad for him, even though I couldn't help but snicker.

"This is perfect. This is exactly how I wanted it.

"Dad, come on, it's broken."

"No, really, I can see the TV perfectly this way." That was Dad, so stubborn. He refused to admit he made an error in judgment, and he never got rid of that lopsided leather chair, which became the "butt" of many family jokes. None of us would admit it, but we all loved that chair.

When my dad's parents came to visit, my grandfather decided to try out the new recliner. He was a shorter man, around five foot seven. He sat down and leaned back and found it fairly comfortable—until my mom called us all for dinner and he couldn't get out. From the kitchen, we heard, "Mama, Mama, come help me!" And my six-foot grandmother went back into the living room to rescue her husband from the cockeyed recliner.

* * *

Dad had a way of turning even the most mundane activity into an over-the-top event. Take sunbathing, for instance. Dad loved to lay out in the backyard, and on the rare occasions when he had time to do so, he followed a particular routine. He would neatly spread out his beach towel on a low canvas lounge chair and carefully oil himself. He always started face up, and when it was time to flip over, he'd ask for help oiling his back. If he was still by the pool in the late afternoon when the sun hung lower in the sky, he would stack bricks on the deck and then prop the head of the chair on the bricks so he could catch just the right angle and make the most of the available sunrays. After spending several hours in the sun, Dad's face was often quite red. If I mentioned this to him, however, he would invariably say, "This is not a sunburn. It's a tan."

Another example: Dad eating eggs. First, he salted those over-easy eggs as if he would never have salt again. While the salt seeped into every inch, Dad buttered his toast. Once a smooth, even coat was applied, he returned to the eggs with a fork and knife, cutting them into strips first and then into small squares. My place at the kitchen table was right next to Dad, and every Sunday morning, I marveled at his workmanship, which to my mind rivaled that of a skilled diamond cutter.

Even if something was a one-time event, Dad turned it into an elaborate experience. For example, staying home sick. Dad rarely caught a cold or the flu. But one Sunday afternoon while I was watching television in the family room, he strolled down the hall, wearing his bathrobe, hair disheveled and cheeks covered with two-day-old stubble. He walked right past the family room into the kitchen, where he grabbed a kitchen chair and then set it down in the middle of the family room, facing the television. He walked back to the kitchen and returned with a standing TV tray and set it in front of the kitchen chair. He made another trip to the kitchen, and this time returned with a square electric frying pan filled with water, which he set on the TV tray. He returned to the kitchen one more time, rustled around in a drawer, and then walked in carrying an extension cord, which he connected to the frying pan and then plugged into the wall. Then he disappeared into his bedroom. During this whole process, he didn't say one word, and I simply watched with fascination.

A few minutes later, he strolled back into the family room, carrying a big towel. He sat down in the kitchen chair, facing the electric pan of now boiling water.

"Dad, whatcha doing?" I finally asked.

"This is going to help me breathe," he said, and then draped the towel over the back of his head, leaned his face toward the water, and extended the rest of the towel out past the frying pan with his arms, creating a canopy. Dad breathed in steam for the next ten to fifteen minutes—not in his bedroom or the bathroom, but right in the middle of the family room where everyone could see him playing his sickness to the hilt.

Living with Dad was always an adventure, and I loved every minute.

* * *

The summer I was sixteen, I started working at my dad's dealership, partly because I had a lot of time on my hands and partly because I wanted to be with my dad. One morning we were driving into work, and I happened to glance at his hand on the steering wheel.

"Dad, how come you're not wearing your rings?" I asked. My dad liked nice jewelry and usually wore two rings on his right hand and his wedding ring on his left.

"Well, they were taken," he replied.

"What do you mean?"

"Something happened the other day when I met a couple who wanted to buy a Cadillac. When I knocked on the hotel door, the guy pulled a gun and told me to move inside."

I sat there, stunned. Dad had driven cars to potential customers before, but this visit obviously didn't go as planned.

Dad continued. "The guy told me to strip naked and get into the bed, and then the woman did the same thing and got in next to me. Then the man took several Polaroid pictures of the woman posing with me in compromising positions. When he was done, he told me to get dressed and said I need to meet him in forty-eight hours with a lot of money. If I didn't, he would send the photos to several newspapers. Before he let me go, he told me to take off my rings."

"Oh my gosh, Dad! What did you do? Did you pay him?"

"No, honey. I called Marc Yates, and we took care of it." Our neighbor Marc was fellow military, and he also happened to be the Lodi chief of police.

"What did you guys do?"

"We drove around the other night, looking for the guy, and we happened to spot the car he had at the hotel where I met the couple. So we followed him until he stopped."

"But how do you know he's not going to use those photographs?"

"He will not be doing anything with those pictures. We took care of it."

"How do you know?"

"Because we scared the living daylights out of him."

My dad, the superhero!

I imagine Marc and my dad, two former military men over six feet tall, enjoyed the challenge of tracking this guy down. Maybe they knew all along they weren't going to arrest him, just scare the shit out of him, which they apparently did.

Dad's next "secret mission," however, had far more serious implications.

Me

For the first month or so after my family moved to Lodi, we lived in a motel across the street from the dealership while our house was being built. My mom made it as comfortable as possible, dividing my parents' "room" from ours, where Les and I shared a double bed and three-year-old Lisa slept in a crib. We also had a small kitchenette, and we bought a cooler for storing food. Mom used a hot plate to heat up simple dinners.

We loved visiting our new house during the building phase. Compared to the motel room, it was open and huge, and we couldn't wait to move in. Mom enjoyed picking out the color scheme and the furniture, and Les and I liked talking about which rooms would be ours and how we would decorate them.

We spent a lot of time in the motel swimming pool, because as we learned immediately, Lodi has hot summers. So, *so* hot. I also spent time next to the air conditioner, watching professional football with my dad. The first time I joined him was a Saturday afternoon during preseason—Hall of Fame game. I walked into the motel room to find Dad sitting on the floor with his back against the foot of the bed, the small television on the floor against the wall.

"Hi, Dad. Can I watch with you?" I asked.

"Sure, honey," he said as he patted the floor next to him. My mom and sisters were in the other part of the room and not interested in football, so I took full advantage of being alone with my dad. He had been working long hours during the week, making the dealership his own.

As a nine-year-old, I didn't know much about football, so I asked a lot of questions.

"Wait. I thought they got farther than that. Why are they going backward?"

"Well, they got a penalty, so the ref has to move the ball back," my dad replied.

"Oh." And then a few minutes later, "Why would he give the ball to a guy that keeps getting tackled?"

"He can throw the ball or hand it off to the runner. Sometimes the runner can't find a hole to run through. You have to make fast decisions, and sometimes they don't work the way you want."

"Oh, I get it."

Even though my dad probably just wanted to watch the game, he patiently answered every question. He never sounded angry or irritated. He never said, "Lori, why don't you go play with your sisters." He seemed to enjoy sharing what he knew.

Watching football with my dad on that tiny television launched my lifelong love of sports, particularly softball, swimming, and tennis. It also cemented my attachment to my dad. I adored him and was in awe that he knew so much about seemingly everything. I loved learning from him and soaked it all in. I also felt like he made things happen. He bought the dealership, moved our family to Lodi, and had a house built. In my nine-year-old mind, I really thought he could do anything, and I wanted to be just like him.

* * *

We moved into our new house just before I started fifth grade at Lakewood Elementary School, which was right across the street. I was nervous and excited about being the new kid, and figured I would make friends quickly, just as I had in Cupertino.

At first, it seemed like I was wrong about becoming friends—with one boy in particular. Tim sat behind me, and he started bugging me almost immediately. He repeatedly pulled on my long blonde hair or threw tiny paper balls at the back of my head. Whenever I told him to stop, he just laughed.

One day when my classmates left for recess, I walked up to my teacher and said, "Mrs. Fields, Tim keeps throwing things at me. I've asked him to stop, but he won't. I don't think he likes me."

"No, Lori, boys do things differently," she said with a smile. "He's doing those things because he likes you."

"Are you sure? I don't understand."

"Yes, boys are funny that way. They do things like that when they like a girl."

I was happy to hear that because I thought Tim was so cute! Not long after, Tim asked me if I would be his girlfriend. Of course, I said yes, and he gave me a bulky ring to wear. Even though the ring was too big, it was so special, and I wrapped the back band with string to make it fit.

During recess and lunch, our group of friends used to meet in the space between the back fence and some trees at the edge of the field. Tim and I would hold hands, but we never tried to kiss. Then one day, our friends decided to play Truth or Dare, a game I had never played before. When it came to Tim, he said "dare."

"You and Lori have to kiss," someone said.

"And it has to be open-mouthed," someone else added.

Tim and I stood up. I was so nervous. We leaned our heads toward each other with our mouths open and touched lips. My eyes were wide open, darting around from Tim to our friends to the trees.

"No, Lori, you have to close your eyes!" one of my friends said, and they all laughed. "You're not supposed to look around when you're kissing."

"Oh," I said, embarrassed. How was I supposed to know? I had never done this before, and my mom certainly didn't talk about boys and kissing!

So we tried again, and this time, I kept my eyes closed tight.

Tim and I remained boyfriend and girlfriend for the rest of fifth grade and all of sixth grade. We worked as crossing guards together, and we'd always sneak in a kiss while we put on our orange vests.

Those years at Lakewood School hold a special place in my childhood. Even today, if I catch the scent of wet asphalt after a rain, I am transported back in time. I can hear my marker landing in the hopscotch square and the slap of my shoes on wet pavement as I hop, and I am filled with a sense of peace and calm.

***

Until sixth grade, I didn't hate math, but I didn't love it either. Then I had Mr. Chappell, and my attitude changed. Math became a subject I truly enjoyed and excelled in.

Within the first month, Mr. Chappell announced that we would have a contest toward the end of the year. "The winner will have a math law named after them until next year's class has a winner," he explained. "But you won't know when the contest is until the day we have it, so be ready!"

I was so excited. I wanted to win this contest, so I made sure I paid attention each day and completed all of my homework.

One morning before we started our first subject, Mr. Chappell stood up and said, "Today is the contest!"

All around the room, students said, "No way!" "Whoa!" "Really?" He had given us hints all year, then sprang it on us out of the blue, just like he said he would.

Mr. Chappell walked to the chalkboard and started writing out fraction problems involving multiplication and division. And he just kept writing. My classmates and I looked at each other in disbelief. The chalkboard was covered. There was no way I could finish all of those problems, and I started feeling uneasy about my chances of winning.

When he finally finished, Mr. Chappell turned around and said, "Okay, the way to win this contest is to write a single paragraph explaining how to solve all of these problems. To win, you must use proper grammar and punctuation. Any questions?"

When no questions came, he instructed us to take out paper and pencil, then said the magic word: "Go!"

I looked at the problems on the board for thirty seconds or so, and then the answer just came to me. I knew it! I wrote out my paragraph, taking care to spell every word correctly and use proper grammar, then I looked around. Most people were still staring at the chalkboard. A few had started writing, but no one else had finished.

I ran up to Mr. Chappell's desk and handed him my paper. As he read it over, I clasped my hands together in front of my chest, just knowing I was right.

"Lori, you have a mistake," Mr. Chappell said as he looked up at me.

"Oh, no. What is it?"

"The first letter of the first word isn't capitalized."

"Oh," I said, so disappointed. I had even indented the paragraph to make it look proper. I turned around and walked slowly back toward my desk, my head drooping toward my chest.

Suddenly, my classmates started yelling, "Lori, change the letter! Hurry, hurry. Change the letter before someone else gets up there!"

I looked up, bewildered. "Really?"

"Come on, Lori, hurry!"

I ran back to my desk and changed the first letter to a capital Y, so the sentence now started, "You multiply or divide..." Then I hurried up to Mr. Chappell's desk and handed him the paper again.

He looked at it and scratched his chin and pretended to give it a lot of thought, and then said, "Lori, you won!"

"I did? Really?"

The whole class clapped and cheered as I beamed. Mr. Chappell handed me the page, stood up, and said, "Lori, read the Law of Lori Peters to the class."

I took a deep breath and read my paragraph. Then, in an official-sounding voice, Mr. Chappell announced, "This will be the Law of Lori Peters until we name next year's winner."

I was so proud and couldn't wait to tell my family. I felt this was the start of something great for me, that my curiosity and ability to figure things out would lead me in a positive direction.

If only that had been true.

* * *

For as long as I could remember, my dad had driven a Cadillac. He had one in Michigan, in Cupertino, and then in Lodi. If a family photo included a car, it was a Cadillac.

When I was eleven, my sisters and I attended a fancy father-daughter luncheon sponsored by Shriners. After we all dressed up and curled our hair, my mom drove us to the dealership to meet my dad. We stood by his latest Cadillac, waiting for him to come out of the building. Soon, a used 1960s four-door Datsun pulled up next to my dad's car. We all stared. There was Dad, dressed in his suit and shiny cufflinks, behind the wheel of this dull old car.

"Dad! What are you doing?" my sister Les said when he stopped. "We can't take this car!"

"Why aren't we taking your Cadillac?" I chimed in.

"Come on, girls, get in. I like this car, and I want to drive it. This is the car we're driving today."

We all piled in, me in my usual seat right behind Dad, but we didn't stop giving him a hard time all the way to the banquet. Of all the days for him to want to drive *this* car!

"What are people going to say when you pull up in this?" Les asked.

"You know, I like this car," my dad replied, "and I don't care what people say. You shouldn't worry about what people say about you or what you want to do."

As he talked, something clicked. I understood what he meant about not caring what people think, and I agreed 100 percent. *I want to be like that*, I thought as I smiled at this new revelation and stopped teasing my dad.

My sisters, however, kept laughing and giving him a hard time. "Stop, you guys," I finally said. "You don't get it."

They didn't stop, but that was okay. I got it. I knew what lesson my dad was trying to teach us, and it made so much sense.

Another time when we were driving around with my dad, we saw garbage collectors out on their route.

"Dad, is it okay to be a garbage man? What if I want to be a garbage man someday?" I asked from the back seat.

"Honey, if you want to be a garbage man, if that's what makes you happy, then that's what you need to do," my dad said. "Just make sure you give it a hundred percent. Whatever you do in life, give it your all. That's what matters."

* * *

When I was in seventh grade, I was sitting in class, listening to the teacher, when I suddenly felt a warm liquid sensation between my legs. I had no idea what was happening, so I raised my hand and asked if I could use the bathroom.

Everyone was in class, so the bathroom was empty, and I hurried into the first stall. I don't remember seeing anything in my underwear, but as I sat on the toilet, I heard slow drips hitting the water. I looked down and saw blood. *Why am I bleeding?* I thought as I started crying. *What is wrong with me?*

At that moment, the bathroom door opened. *Oh, my gosh. I can't believe someone is coming in now!* Through the gap next to the stall door, I could see that it was a teacher's assistant. *Okay, Lori, get yourself together and go back to class. Maybe you figure this out when you get home.*

I pulled up my underwear, took a deep breath, and opened the door. The woman stood at the mirror, touching up her makeup. She looked back at me and could tell I had been crying. "What's the matter? Is something wrong?" she asked.

I figured I might as well tell her, so I said, "I'm bleeding. I think something's really wrong with me."

"Where are you bleeding?"

I tapped the front of my dress in the center above my legs.

"Oh sweetie, there's nothing wrong with you," she said. "You're becoming a woman. That happens to every girl when they become a woman. You will bleed once a month now."

"Really?" I asked. I couldn't believe what I was hearing. My mom had never told me this would happen! I was angry about finding out this way and embarrassed about thinking something was really wrong.

"Here, let me take you to the office. We can call your mom so she can come pick you up. That way you can change your clothes."

Oh, great. Mom's going to come pick me up. How's that going to go? I thought. *What will she even say?*

Sure enough, the car ride home was nearly silent. I just stared out the window while my mom drove the mile or so to our house.

When we got home, I headed straight to the bathroom. "Wait right here," my mom said. "I'm going to get you something."

She walked down the hall to her bedroom and shut the door behind her. A minute later, she came out and headed toward me with something in her hand. "I thought this was going to happen soon," she said. "I was going to give this to you before your dad and I left on our trip." She handed me a pad and an elastic strap device. "This is what you can wear."

That was it. No explanation or demonstration. She turned and walked back to her bedroom. I looked down at the contraption and thought, *What the hell is this?* as I walked into the bathroom. It was one of those old-school period belts, with an elastic strap that went around your waist and short straps that hung down from the front and back of the waist, and I couldn't figure out how to wear it without it appearing bulky. After a few minutes, I gave up. I threw the elastic thing across the room, put the pad in my underwear, and went back to my bedroom.

When Les got home, I went to her room, held out the contraption, and said, "Mom gave me this. What is it?"

"Yeah, she gave me one of those too," Les said. "Here, follow me."

She walked across the hall to the bathroom and opened a cabinet under the sink closest to the toilet. She pulled out a box of Tampax and took out a tampon. "These are much easier to use. You just put it in, to about here," she said as she pointed to the cardboard tube, "and then push on the smaller part. There's instructions on the box if you have a problem."

So I didn't have to wear that elastic thing after all. *Thank goodness!*

Talking to Les about my period was a little awkward, because my family didn't talk about personal things like that, but I knew Les would know what to do. Though she looked the most like our mother, she couldn't have been more different personality-wise. Les was bold and brash and very much her own person. She regularly made comments just to get a reaction out of my mom, and she had mastered the art of quick comebacks in an argument. When Les and I fought, it was about the usual sister stuff—I borrowed a shirt without asking or disagreed with her—but I always knew she would be there for me if I was desperate and needed her, like when my period started and later when I needed advice about boys and sex.

My sister Lisa, on the other hand, looked the most like my dad but shared my mom's personality. Because she was much younger than Les and me, she often felt left out of our activities and turned to my mom for attention. Mom, in turn, babied her, making special meals separate from what the rest of the family ate. Lisa was adorable, with bright blonde hair and a cute little nose.

I resembled both parents, but I shared my dad's sense of humor, inquisitive nature, and desire to learn and improve. Like Dad, I thought about what I might be when I grew up. From a very young age, it became clear that I am my father's daughter.

* * *

When I was around twelve, Dad took me with him to look at some property in the foothills. The businessman gave us each a horse to ride the short distance to the land. On the way back, the businessman galloped his horse in, and I was itching to do the same.

"Go ahead, Lori," my dad said. "You can run him." He knew how much I loved horses. I had ridden bareback ponies many times, and I was very much at home on horseback.

"Thanks, Dad!" I said and then took off. Oh, how I loved that feeling of flying on horseback! I met the businessman at the trailer, and we waited for my dad, who trotted in, bouncing up and down, up and down.

"Come on, Dad," I yelled. "Just ride him in!"

But he just kept trotting along, this big guy on a big horse looking very uncomfortable, perhaps because he hadn't ridden a horse since he was a teen.

After he finally arrived, we put the horses back in the trailer and met the businessman at a local cafe. As soon as the waitress cleared the dishes, my dad wrote some numbers on a napkin and slid it across the table to the businessman, who wrote something down and passed the napkin back. Finally, the two men shook hands, and the businessman stood.

"I'll be in touch," he said, and then left the cafe.

"So, did everything go okay?" I asked my dad.

"Yeah, we made a deal."

"What do you mean?"

He pointed to the napkin. "Right here, we made a deal."

"Dad, you can't make a deal on a napkin."

"Sure you can. You can make a deal on any piece of paper. You just have to both sign it and shake hands, and the deal is done."

"Really?" This fascinated me. I assumed the deal had to be an official-looking typed document. Dad regularly surprised me with his knowledge and humor, and I always wanted more.

Mom, on the other hand, kept her knowledge close and did things on her own. She cleaned the whole house, our rooms included; my sisters and I were only responsible for making sure everything was off the floor. If I asked what I could do to help, she might hand me a feather duster, almost reluctantly. Dusting didn't take too long, so I'd come back and ask, "What else can I do?"

"Oh, that's it, thanks."

She had a certain way of doing almost everything, and she wanted to take care of it on her own rather than take time to explain how she wanted it done. She did the laundry, ironed, sewed hems or fixed loose buttons, and cooked dinner, but she didn't include me in the chores or teach me how to do those things for myself. To me, these were lost opportunities to connect, and their absence saddened me.

* * *

For the most part, I was a good student who kept out of trouble. I had never been disciplined or sent to detention. I had never even been in the counselor's office. Then, when I was in eighth grade, I received a summons to see the school counselor immediately. All the way from my classroom to the office, I wondered what I could have done.

I walked in, and the secretary pointed me upstairs toward an open door. As I walked in, I saw the counselor sitting behind her desk, looking very prim and proper with her tailored suit and perfectly styled dark hair. For a second, I thought, *Wow, she looks just like my mom*—and simultaneously sensed we weren't the only ones in the room. I looked behind me and saw Mom sitting in a chair, looking equally prim and proper, her hands neatly folded in her lap. She didn't say a word as I walked in. *Oh no. This isn't going to be good*, I thought.

The counselor stood and said, "Hi, Lori. I want to show you something. Why don't you have a seat."

"Okay," I mumbled as I took the only vacant chair, which was closer to the counselor's desk than to my mom.

The counselor walked over and handed me a piece of paper. "Is this your writing?" she asked.

No, no, no! I thought. *How can she have this?* It was a note I had been passing back and forth with my friend the day before, one in which I talked about what I had been doing with my boyfriend, Sam. Nothing serious—we had recently started exploring a little—but in this note, I told my friend about kissing Sam and the fact that he had touched my boob.

"Yes, this is my writing," I told the counselor, trying to keep the panic out of my voice.

"Why did you write this? Are you doing these things?"

"No, no. I was just joking around. I would say things to my friend, she would say things back. I'm not doing these things."

"Well, I hope not," my mom said tightly, the only words she spoke during the entire meeting.

"No, I'm not."

"Well, okay," said the counselor. "Lori, you can go back to class. I'm going to talk to your mom a bit."

My mom didn't say goodbye, and we never talked about the incident again. She never brought it up because that would mean she would have to talk to me about sex, which I knew wouldn't happen. She didn't talk to me about my period, so there was no way she'd talk to me about sex.

Though Sam and I continued exploring, I never wrote another note about it. I knew I wouldn't get away with lying a second time.

Sam and I became boyfriend and girlfriend when he was in seventh grade and I was in eighth. I was taller than him, and I used to carry his saxophone when we walked home from school together. Sometimes we took a detour and walked around Lodi Lake, which separated Woodbridge School from my neighborhood.

My parents knew I was seeing Sam, and my dad used to tease me about him. Sam had wispy blonde hair that hung down just right to showcase his blue eyes. I used to describe him as foxy.

When we took a family vacation to Hawaii, my dad and I often walked together on the beach. Whenever he saw a boy around my age, he'd say, "Hey, Lori, is that guy foxy like Sam?"

"No, Dad. *Sam* is foxy."

"How about that one?"

I'd laugh and say, "No, Dad, I like Sam."

"Oh, that's right, Sam is foxy!" Dad would say with a mischievous grin.

Whenever Sam and I went to the movies, he would put his arm around my shoulders, and sometimes he'd try to slip his hand under my shirt. The problem was that I was a lot taller. He'd inch up in his chair until he could finally slip his hand down my shirt and under my bra, but I could tell Sam was uncomfortable. After thirty seconds or so, his hand would return to my shoulder. Even so, I felt so grown up when he touched me like that, and I tingled all over.

One night, we were watching a movie when the film suddenly stopped and the theater owner appeared on the platform in front of the screen.

"You kids need to quiet down!" he yelled. "People paid good money to watch this film, and you're being too loud."

Unfortunately, the owner was short in stature and not very intimidating. The kids in the audience didn't take him seriously; some laughed, and others shouted, "Start the movie!"

Then, the owner pulled out a gun and started waving it around while yelling, "Be quiet! Shut up! I'm not going to restart this movie until you shut up!"

Some kids were shocked into silence; others started yelling even more. "What are you going to do, shoot us?"

At that point, some kids got up and left, and Sam and I joined them. In the lobby, I used the payphone to call my dad. I told him what happened, and Dad drove straight to the theater as soon as he hung up. Through the lobby windows, I watched him park his car, get out, and stride toward the building, long black trench coat flapping like Superman's cape behind him.

"Are you okay?" Dad asked when he reached us. We nodded.

"Where is the owner now? What type of gun did he have?"

"I don't know. It was small," I replied. "I think he's still in the theater."

Dad told us to wait in the lobby, and then he marched into the theater. I could tell the owner was in big trouble.

About ten minutes later, Dad reappeared and said, "Let's go."

We followed him to the car and got in. "What happened?" I asked.

"I had a little talk with him."

"What did you say?"

"It's taken care of. He'll never do anything like that again."

Of course, I wanted to know more, but I didn't press him since Sam was there. What I would have given to see my hero in action!

* * *

"Where are you going?" my mom asked from the kitchen. *Dang it!* I had tried to sneak out the backdoor to the garage, but no such luck.

"I'm just going to a friend's house," I said.

"Well, don't you think you should put on your bra?" That was exactly why I had tried to sneak out. I knew she would have something to say.

"No, I don't feel like it. I'm just going to my friend's. I'll be back."

The truth was that I was going to see Sam, and I wanted to show off my figure a little. I had on a lightweight maroon sweater with jeans, and not wearing a bra made me feel more womanly and attractive.

I walked across the street so I could take the shortcut through Lakewood School. As I entered the parking lot, an elderly couple pulled up to ask for directions.

"Oh sure," I said. "Keep going straight and then turn right at the stop sign."

"Thank you," they said together.

After they drove off, I continued walking through the parking lot, feeling happy that I was able to help them out. I walked across the sports field to Turner Road on the other side of the school. A few minutes later, a white pickup truck pulled over to the curb next to me. The driver was a good-looking guy in his thirties. He rolled down the passenger side window, leaned across the seat, and said,

"Hey, can you give me directions to the mall?"

This is crazy, I thought. *Is everyone lost today?*

"Sure," I said. "Just keep going straight down Turner Road. It will curve around, and then you make a right. You can't miss it."

"Okay," he said. "But I'm running late to a meeting, and I want to make sure I get there. I don't know this area. Do you think you could come with me, and then I'll bring you right back?"

I told him I didn't have time to do that, so he asked for directions again. I repeated them, but as I did, I sensed that something wasn't right. These were very simple instructions. We lived in a small town, and there was only one mall. What didn't he understand?

After I finished, he said, "I'm sorry, I just can't hear you. Can you come a little closer?" I walked toward the passenger door a little, thinking, *This is the last time I'm going to say this.*

"You just keep going down this street..." I raised my arm as I spoke, pointing and looking toward the mall. Suddenly, the guy slid across the seat, stuck his arm out the window, and lifted up my sweater. I slammed my arm down on his arm as hard as I could. He let go and started laughing. Then slid back across the seat and took off.

I was in complete shock. I felt so embarrassed. I also felt guilty, like I caused this situation by not wearing a bra. I kept thinking of my conversation with my mom before I left and knew there was no way I could ever tell her what happened. Whereas Dad always took my side, Mom tended to take the other person's side and assumed that I was at fault, and this would only prove her point—especially after the note-writing incident in the counselor's office.

I wished I could have talked to my mom about Sam and sex and what happened with the guy in the truck, but to me, she made it clear that she didn't want to. I couldn't talk to my dad because girls didn't talk to their fathers about such things. I hated that I had to find out important, personal information from Les, my friends, even my teacher, rather than her.

* * *

When I was in junior high, I had two best friends, and they were as different as night and day. Lori and I became friends in sixth grade. She came from a close Baptist family that went to church together every Sunday. She had long brown hair that framed her face and a full, pouty lower lip, before that became a thing. Stylish and sweet as sugar, Lori brought out the lady in me, while I made her laugh with my quick wit.

Debbie, on the other hand, had a difficult home life. Her parents drank and smoked, and her mother had a hard look that told me not to get on her bad side. Debbie mostly kept to herself, but after we became close friends in seventh grade, she opened up with me and displayed an inner strength I admired.

On a beautiful sunny Saturday afternoon in April 1974, I met Lori and Debbie at Lakewood Elementary School for one of our regular girl chats. Though we were in junior high, we often met at Lakewood because we all lived within a short walking distance. It was a natural meeting place to talk about boys, our upcoming graduation, and other hot topics.

On this particular Saturday, I mainly wanted to talk about Sam. I would be moving on to high school, while he had one more year in junior high, and I was worried we might stop seeing each other.

After talking a bit, I blurted out, "I want to marry Sam. Do you guys want to get married someday?"

"I don't think we will have time to get married," Lori said. That seemed like such a strange answer, and I started laughing.

"What?" I asked. "What do you mean?"

"We won't have time because God is coming down to earth to take everyone up to heaven."

"Lori, what are you talking about?" I said. "You're joking, right?"

"No, I'm not joking. The Second Coming is happening."

"What is the Second Coming?"

"Well, God doesn't like what's happening on earth, and he's coming to take everyone with him up to heaven."

Confused, I looked at Debbie and asked, "What is Lori talking about? Do you believe this? Do you know about the Second Coming?"

"Oh yeah. It's just like Lori said."

Still not believing what I was hearing, I asked them, "Who told you this? How long have you known God is coming?"

"As long as I can remember," Lori said. "My parents told me when I was really young."

"I've always known, too," Debbie said.

They both looked at me for a second, surprised, as if this information was common knowledge. "Your parents never told you about the Second Coming?" Lori finally asked.

As soon as the question left Lori's mouth, I felt the weight of her words and the meaning behind them. This moment was going to change everything—I just knew it.

"No, they never told me," I replied. More secrets, something else I had to find out from someone other than my parents.

Thoughts raced through my mind. *Do my parents know about the Second Coming? Why didn't they tell me? My friends are actually serious. They both believe this, so it must be true.* I started to panic inside, but I couldn't let my friends see my fear, so I kept asking questions.

"So, how do you know God is coming *soon*?" I asked.

"Tom started working part time at *Lodi News Sentinel*," Lori said, referring to her older brother. "The newspaper is ready to print the story on the front page with the headline 'The Second Coming Is Here.' Tom told me his coworkers are so excited because God is already showing signs that he is coming. They are waiting for more signs from God before they print the story on the front page."

"What signs?" Even as I asked, I knew I was digging myself in deeper, but I had to know what was coming.

"The wars and earthquakes we've been having. The signs to come are that summer will turn into winter, and winter will turn into summer. You won't be able to tell what month it is. All the animals will start behaving strangely. There are more signs, too, and after they all happen, the sky will break open, and God will appear. He will come down from heaven and ask everyone a question."

I tried to picture what Lori described. My heart pounded, and fear clenched my gut, though I didn't let it show.

"What question is God going to ask?" I asked.

"God will ask everyone if they want to go to heaven with him," Lori said.

My curiosity turned to defiance.

"Well, I don't want to go. I want to stay here. I don't want to die. I want to get married. I want to have kids. Don't you want to get married? Have kids? You know you will die if you go with God."

"I want to go with God when he comes," Lori said.

"Me too," Debbie agreed. "It will be great. I can't wait."

"Neither can I," Lori said. "It will be so wonderful to be with God. We get to live with him. Heaven is a beautiful place."

Who are my friends? Why do they want to die? I don't want to die!

"I want to stay here," I said. "I want to have a life. I don't want to go."

"Well, you can say no to God," Lori said. In the split second that she paused, I thought, *I can? Then that's what I'll do!*

Then Lori continued: "But if you say no and your family says yes to God, you will be here all alone. You will never see your family again."

My stomach dropped. "Why?"

"Because you won't be able to change your mind. If you decide later that you want to go live with God, you won't be able to. You will have to stay here on earth with everyone else who says no."

"What happens to the people on earth who say no?"

"Everyone who says no will have a mark of 666 on their forehead, and that mark is permanent," Debbie replied. "It will never come off. That way, everyone will always know your decision. And everything on earth will look and be different. You won't recognize anything. There'll be many more wars, and people will kill each other. No matter what happens to the earth in the future, you will never be able to leave, so you have to make sure you make the right decision."

Lori and Debbie answered every question without hesitation. They knew exactly what would happen. They both seemed so eager to give me all the facts and "help" me understand—that I couldn't show my true feelings of utter despair. *Have my parents been protecting me from this?* I wondered.

Somewhere in my mind, a blinking neon sign started flashing: *This. Is. All. True.* Yet I couldn't wrap my brain around the fact that God was coming soon, and I could either go with him and die or choose to stay on an unrecognizable earth forever. And either way, I might be all alone. *How can I be sure what my family's answer will be? I could be separated from my family forever.*

Between the flashing sign and the unbearable choice I would have to make, my mind felt completely overpowered by fear and dread. Suddenly, I felt and heard something in my brain shift to the left and to the right, and then settle back into place. I slowly looked up at my two best friends. I saw them, but not clearly. They were still speaking, but I could hardly hear them. I drifted into another reality filled with fog. I felt that if I were to reach out to touch my friends, they would just disappear in a cloud of dust.

I didn't know what was happening to me. All I could think of was getting home. *I have to try and stop the bleeding. Run home. Run, Lori, run home.*

I turned and started running, while yelling, "I have to go!" I knew I was running, but I didn't feel my feet hit the pavement. I just kept thinking, *Run home. Run, Lori, run home.*

Lori and Debbie may have called after me as I ran, but I didn't hear them. I was focused on running.

Can I even open our big front door? I wondered as I turned the knob. I didn't think I had the strength, but the door opened, and I ran to my bedroom. I hurriedly closed the door and collapsed on my bed. I cried for what seemed like hours, trying to wrap my brain around what I had discovered. My mind whirled with thoughts, conclusions, strategies, and dreads. My brain couldn't keep up. I was utterly exhausted. *Lori, just try to sleep. Close your eyes, sleep.* But I couldn't sleep. I started pacing around my bedroom. *What are you going to do?* I kept asking myself.

Then in the next heartbeat, I thought, *This can't be true.*

But you know it is, I answered immediately. *I'm not going to be able to get married or have kids. I'm going to die soon. How long do I have? Days? A month? A year?*

I shook my head back and forth, saying one word quietly but emphatically: "Nooooo!"

I dropped to the floor and leaned against the foot of my bed. I became angry. *No!* I thought. *I'm not going to let this happen. God is not going to find me. If he doesn't find me, he can't ask me that* question. *It's just not going to happen. I'm not going to believe the Second Coming is happening. Lori, you'll have to come up with a plan—and soon.*

Suddenly I heard Mom yelling for us to come eat dinner. *What? It's dinnertime already?* I had been in my room for hours.

Okay. Lori, pull yourself together. You can't let your family suspect anything is wrong. You're not sure if they even know about the Second Coming, so protect them and yourself. Put on your best game face.

"Coming, Mom!" I yelled as I opened my bedroom door. Under my breath, I thought, *Game on, killer.*

My Dad

By late 1976, Dad's business had completely overcome the slump caused by the oil crisis. Since taking ownership six years earlier, he had boosted overall sales by 392 percent, and during the same period, his dealership—by then called Peters Pontiac-Cadillac-GMC-Fiat—was the largest Cadillac distributor in California.

Success like that attracts attention, sometimes the unwanted kind.

In June 1977, a local real estate developer named Elmer Bertsch walked into my dad's office and said, "I have some people that want to buy your agency."[1]

---

1 Andrew Dubbins, "When the Mafia Came to Lodi," Alta, December 19, 2020, https://www.altaonline.com/dispatches/a34977139/mafia-joe-bonanno-lodi-lou-peters/. I'm grateful to Dubbins for his diligent research. Dad didn't talk about this secret during the years he was involved with the FBI, and Dubbins's article filled in so many details. I've relied on it heavily for this chapter, along with my dad's personal notebook, discussions with Bob Anderson and Carl Larsen, the transcript of an interview with the FBI after his undercover work ended, and the transcript of Dad's last call with Joe Bonanno Sr.

"It's not for sale," Dad told him.

"Name any price. They've got all kinds of money."

My dad figured the dealership was worth around $1 million, so to rid himself of an unwanted buyer, he doubled the number and said, "$2 million."

A couple of days later, Elmer returned and said, "They said $2 million is okay."

Dad asked who was behind the deal, but Elmer said they wanted to remain anonymous. This piqued Dad's interest as to who would be willing to pay double and why. My dad kept pushing until Elmer finally asked, "Have you ever heard of Joe Bonanno Sr.?"

"No."

"He's the head of the Mafia for the whole United States."

Dad was stunned and wondered what the Mafia was doing in a nice place like Lodi. He told the developer that he wanted to deal with these people directly, so Elmer set up a meeting for a few days later.

In Dad's personal notebook, he wrote, "June 14, 1977: first meeting with Bill Bonanno," referring to Salvatore, the eldest of Joe Sr.'s two sons. He also met with Joe Jr. in that first discussion, and together the Bonannos laid out their plans. In addition to the $2 million from the sale, they offered to pay Dad $100,000 a year to identify and purchase twelve to fourteen California car dealerships. The Bonannos would supervise the operations and provide the cash, but my dad's name would be on the paperwork.

As he listened to Bill and Joe Jr., my dad realized what they were proposing: they wanted to launder money through the dealerships, with Dad as their front man.

After his one and only experience in jail for siphoning gas, Dad had become an honest, hardworking businessman. He wanted no part of the Mafia's scheme, but he also knew they would find another dealer, so using his brilliant negotiating skills, he kept Bill and Joe Jr. on the hook and left the meeting without giving them an answer. Dad also wanted to verify whether the brothers were truly Mafia. After the meeting, he drove straight to Lodi police chief Marc Yates's house and told him the whole story.

"Oh my God," Marc said. "This could cause all kinds of problems for our community."

Marc called the FBI's Stockton office, and they set up a meeting between Dad, Marc, Dad's attorney, and an FBI agent. Once the agent verified my dad's story, special agent Bob Anderson took the lead on the case.

In the past, Bob had handled interstate crimes like moving stolen property, but never a case involving organized crime. Of course, he had heard of Joe Bonanno. The "Old Man," as he was nicknamed, was the boss of one of New York's infamous Five Families. Although Joe Sr. had been investigated for various crimes, including illegal gambling and heroin trafficking, and was suspected of putting hits on several rivals, the FBI had never managed to collect enough evidence against him. At that point in 1977, Bonanno was living in Tucson, Arizona, "retired" from his life of crime.

Bob invited my dad to meet him and four other agents at his Stockton office, where Dad identified one of the Bonanno brothers based on photos. Then Bob asked him a question that changed his life, and that of our whole family: "Would you be willing to go undercover to gather information on the Bonannos?"

Bob told him up front that the operation could take years and that it would be extremely dangerous. "If you're discovered, Bonanno has the ability to hunt you down and kill you, Lou."

Dad told Bob that he needed to talk to my mom, but in truth, he had already made up his mind. One of Dad's childhood dreams was to become an FBI agent, and now he had a chance to do the next best thing.

Mom was understandably scared and asked Dad why he wanted to do this. "If I don't, who will?" he replied.

The next morning Dad called Bob Anderson and said, "I'm in. Let's do this."

"Okay, let's do this," Bob said.

"I just have one request," Dad continued. "Do not call me an informant." He hated that word and all that it implied. Informants are usually criminals who are trying to cut a deal. They provide information in exchange for a lesser sentence and/or money. Dad made it very clear that he would not take money. He was participating in this operation because it was the right thing to do.

"Okay, we'll never refer to you as an informant," Bob said. "We'll call you a 'concerned citizen.'"

Many years later, Bob told me that this was the one lie he told my dad. In all the FBI files, Bob had to document that Dad was an informant, since that was the only way for him to legally receive FBI protection.

After recruiting my dad, Bob discovered that the Old Man had $40 million in Canada under the care of a Bonanno *capo* (captain). When Bonanno died, however, the money could be seized by the Canadian government. To prevent that from happening, Bonanno sought to launder the money through US businesses with heavy cash flow, like car dealerships.

In early August 1977, Dad met with Bill Bonanno to finalize their agreement regarding the sale of the dealership. By that point, Dad had started wearing a wire to record in-person conversations, and the FBI had also installed a special phone in a locked drawer in Dad's office. Dad presented himself as a businessman who had no problem accepting Mafia money. Before it was final, however, Bill needed the Old Man to sign off. Dad recorded Bill's exact words: "I don't make a move without my father knowing."

On August 22, 1977, my dad met with the Old Man for the first time, writing in his notebook, "First meeting with Mr. Bonanno,

Sr." The Old Man was impressed by Dad's success and felt he'd make a good business partner for Bill. At the end of the meeting, he put one hand on his son's shoulder and one on my dad's. "I'm glad you two got together," he said in his thick Sicilian accent. "You'll both make a lot of money."

Since General Motors owned 40 percent of the dealership, Dad had to get the sale approved before it was final. Bob and Dad flew to Detroit to talk with General Motors' executives, who ultimately voted not to authorize the sale. They were concerned about bad publicity, legal liability, and the safety of employees at a Mafia-owned dealership.

Despite this setback, my dad tried to learn more about the Bonannos' money laundering scheme, since his ultimate goal was to bring it to an end and see the family imprisoned. Dad sold three cars to Bonanno family associates and three to Bill's family. He also sold a few cars for Bill, including Bill's own maroon Cadillac with cloth seats. My dad reported everything to Bob, who coached him on the kinds of money laundering evidence they needed and that were permitted in court.

One of Dad's ideas to get evidence involved enticing Bill and the Old Man's nephew, Jack DiFilippi, into a business venture that involved customizing Pontiacs and selling them under the name Barchetta. A few months earlier, the Barchetta took first place in the sport coupe category at the 1977 Sacramento Autorama, and Dad was in negotiations with General Motors on customizing designs before the Mafia came calling. My dad told Bill and Jack that the dealership had been flooded with orders for Barchettas and offered to sell them—with the Old Man's approval—the patent and distribution rights for $1 million.

In September 1977, Jack called our house, and my sister Les answered. Jack introduced himself as someone who worked with our dad and suggested that our families all get together some time for dinner. When Dad found out, he blew up and told Bob he needed to get a legal separation to protect mom, my sisters, and me.

"It's not expected," Bob told him. "No one would ever ask you [to do that]."

"I'm just stating what I'm going to do," Dad replied. He didn't wait for FBI approval. He decided a legal separation was the best way to keep his family safe, so that was what he was going to do. That still didn't make it easy. In a later interview with the FBI, Dad stated, "The hardest part was telling the girls." He took us aside individually and explained that the separation was for business purposes only and that it was temporary.

Bob found a two-story apartment complex in Stockton that was perfect for the operation. He rented a lower-level apartment for Dad and the one directly above it for himself. The FBI installed surveillance equipment throughout my dad's apartment, the most elaborate setup in the country at that time. They bugged the kitchen, bedroom, phone, living room—everything but the bathroom. They dismantled the fireplace upstairs in Bob's apartment and lowered a man into the chimney headfirst to build shelves and install video equipment in Dad's apartment. They set up two video cameras, one in the living room behind a large floral metal art piece on the fireplace, and the other in the dining room behind a tiger painting, with the lens in the tiger's eye.

My dad spent many lonely nights in that apartment, but he viewed it as a tour of duty, not unlike his service in the Marines. He was a patriot through and through.

He also found ways to make apartment living fun, mainly by pranking Bob upstairs. Bob's girlfriend, Judy, sometimes spent the night, and when she did, Dad had a little fun at their expense. He would wait until he thought Bob and Judy were in bed having sex, and then call.

"Hello?" Bob would say.

"Oh, I just wanted to say hi," Dad would respond and then hang up, repeating the prank a couple times.

One time, Dad and Bob were preparing for a meeting with Jack in my dad's apartment. Upstairs, Bob turned on the video and sound equipment to make sure it was working. As Bob watched on the monitors, Dad walked through the apartment, naked. Bob stomped on the floor, and my dad turned his bare backside toward the camera, then strolled out to get dressed. When the agents later reviewed the tape, they, too, caught a glimpse of Dad's rear end.

Over the next year or so, Dad's cover was almost blown a few times. Once, Jack, who was always suspicious, scoured the apartment looking for surveillance equipment. As he looked right at one of the cameras a few feet away, he said, "I think your place might be wired."

"Well, if you think it's wired, let's get the hell out of here!" Dad said. "That makes me nervous."

Another time, when my dad was wearing a wire under his sports coat on a very hot day, Jack insisted that Dad take off the jacket. Bob heard this and made a quick call to the apartment. When Dad answered, Bob gave him a story to tell Jack: "The person on the phone is a woman you have been trying to seduce, and she is available *right now.*" My dad hung up, told Jack the lie, and escaped with his coat on.

* * *

In the spring of 1978, Bill and Joe Jr. were both found guilty of violating their probation. Before they went back to prison, the Old Man traveled from Tucson to San Jose to see his sons. Dad noted, "March 3, 1978: Second meeting with Bonanno Sr. Met in San Jose for dinner at the La Baron. Bill and Joe Jr. were there as well. Discussed probation violation, *Parade* article (insert of the *Sacramento Bee*), and the auto agency purchase will have to wait."[2] As part of his effort to gain the Bonannos' trust, Dad even attended one of Bill's court hearings to show his support.

---

2   The Old Man gave my dad a signed copy of the *Parade* article, in which he bragged about the fact that the FBI had never caught him.

After his sons went back to prison, the Old Man stayed in San Jose for a few months and met my dad on several occasions. In April 1978, Joe Sr. accepted an invitation to visit the dealership, and Dad walked him around the showroom and the rest of the dealership property, as well as the Barchetta.

I happened to stop by the dealership that day because I needed to ask Dad about something. As I waited for him to finish a meeting, I saw him walking through the showroom with a shorter gray-haired older gentleman.

"Hi, Dad," I said as they walked toward me.

"Lori, I want to introduce you to someone," my dad said, turning slightly toward the man next to him. "This is my middle daughter, Lori."

I held out my hand to shake his with confidence, as Dad had taught me, and the man took it warmly in both of his.

"Hello, Lori," he said, soft-spoken and sincere. "Nice to meet you."

"Sorry, Lori, we have to go," Dad said. "We have some business to take care of."

"Oh, sure. Well, it was nice meeting you," I said to the older gentleman, who nodded and then walked off with Dad. I realized after they left that my dad hadn't given me the man's name, which seemed odd.

After they left the dealership that day, my dad took the Old Man to the apartment in Stockton. On the drive, Dad turned up his roleplaying. "You know, my dad came from the old country," he told Bonanno. "There's a lot of mannerisms and things you do that are just like him." He paused. "My dad, as you know, passed away a couple of years ago. You're like a second father to me."

My grandfather came from Greece, not Italy, and years later, in an interview with the FBI, my dad stated, "The resemblance of [Bonanno's] mannerisms and my father's was like a jackass and a human being." In the car, however, the Old Man seemed to believe my dad and was pleased by the comparison.

Some time after Dad and the Old Man arrived at the apartment, Bob Anderson realized the Nagra recorder was running out of tape. He called the apartment and told Dad to tell the Old Man he had to go back to the dealership to sign some papers. My dad did so, but first he drove to a coffee shop off Highway 99 in Lodi to meet Carl Larsen, the lead FBI technician responsible for setting up the surveillance equipment. After he parked, Dad got into the passenger seat of Carl's car and unzipped his pants to reveal the Nagra, taped to the right side of his groin area. Carl leaned over the space between them and carefully replaced the tape and batteries without disturbing the wires.

"Carl," my Dad joked. "If the Lodi PD pulls into this parking lot for coffee, we're going to be in big trouble!"

* * *

The longer Dad worked as a "concerned citizen," the more worried the FBI became that his cover would be blown. After one out-of-town meeting with Jack, my dad returned to his hotel room to find that someone had gone through his briefcase. Then someone made an anonymous phone call to the FBI, saying he knew there was an informant in the Bonanno organization and that the "rat would be murdered."

Perhaps the most frightening incident for Bob was when Dad traveled with Jack and Bill to Miami to meet a potential Barchetta investor. The FBI arranged for Bob to be on the same flight so he could keep an eye on Dad. When they were in the boarding area, however, Jack, Bill, and my dad suddenly stood up and walked away. Bob had no choice but to take the scheduled flight and hope my dad was safe. He didn't have time to call for backup, and only a handful of FBI agents knew about this whole operation in the first place.

When he arrived in Miami, Bob checked into the hotel and then went down to the lobby bar to wait. Three hours later, to Bob's great relief, my dad, Jack, and Bill walked through the lobby. Dad saw Bob at the bar but walked right on by, showing no emotion. Later, Dad called to check in with Bob and explained that Jack had changed flights and made a stop in north Florida to make sure no one was following them.

The next night, my dad was supposed to meet the investor at the wharf. Bob explained that the FBI couldn't follow Dad down the wharf without being spotted, and that it would be too dangerous for him to go through with it.

"I recommend that you refuse and say 'to hell with the case,'" Bob told him. "Your life is more important."

But my dad, my hero, insisted that he go. Bob knew there was no point in trying to change his mind, so he watched Dad enter the wharf area by car and then broke off surveillance. An hour later, Dad, Jack, Bill, and the investor emerged and drove to a restaurant for dinner. Because my dad was wired, the FBI gathered outstanding intelligence from the conversations he had that weekend.

In September 1978, Dad attended a conference in Los Angeles. Before he left, he talked with Bob about visiting the Old Man in Tucson after the conference ended. Dad wanted to wear the usual Nagra recorder so he could change the tape and be sure to capture everything, but Bob told him it would be too dangerous to wear a wire in Bonanno's home. Dad reluctantly agreed. Score one for Bob. The truth was, my dad had a remarkable memory during those times he wasn't able to wear a wire.

When Dad arrived at the Old Man's home in Tucson, he was greeted warmly, with the traditional cheek kiss. The Old Man introduced Dad to his wife, Fay, and gave him a tour of the house, including his office. Then they went for a walk, and the Old Man told Dad that he had discovered his house was bugged.

"It's being handled," the Old Man said. He was desperate to get his sons out of prison and told Dad he intended to find out who was targeting his family.

Dad purposely hadn't booked a hotel, hoping the Old Man would offer him a place to stay, which he did. As the chauffeur drove my dad to the guest house, he said, "Don't you know you're part of the family?" The next morning, in another effort to look loyal and trustworthy in the Old Man's eyes, my dad visited Joe Jr. in prison south of Phoenix.

Despite the information my dad had gathered, as of November 1978, the operation hadn't yielded any usable evidence, and Bob's FBI supervisor in Washington DC was becoming impatient. Bob spent hours writing reports listing the reasons they should keep it going. He detailed the numerous people they had connected to the Mafia, and he accused the FBI of abandoning my dad. These reports bought them a couple more months, but in January 1979, the investigation was officially closed. Dad was disappointed. He felt he had failed and wanted to keep the investigation going.

The next step was to figure out how to "extract" Dad from the operation and sever his ties with the Bonannos. Bob and Dad thought about a fake heart attack, since my dad had suffered two in 1975. Then the FBI suggested that they have my dad subpoenaed to appear before the federal grand jury.

"No, I don't want to go before the federal grand jury," Dad told them at first. "Then there will be nineteen more people who know what I've been doing."

In the end, Dad decided a subpoena was the way to go. "I might as well get this thing over with and do it right," he told Bob.

On February 15, 1979, Dad was served with an official subpoena. He went into his office at the dealership and called the Old Man on the secret phone. Worried that the FBI might be eavesdropping, the Old Man left his house and called Dad back from a payphone. Of course, that didn't matter, since Dad's office phone was bugged.

"I hate to bother you, but this morning I was served with a subpoena," my dad said. "There are some things they're going to ask me, and I want to be sure what to do."

"Ahhh," was all the Old Man said.

Dad continued: "Subpoena is for the 22nd of February at Room 17207, Golden Gate Avenue, US District Court Grand Jury. And let's see...this subpoena was used on the application of United States, Craig A. Starr."

"Yes, it's the same guy," the Old Man said.

"Oh, you know him?"

"The guy who sent the boys over there."

"Oh, that's the son of a bitch?"

"Yeah."

Dad then told the Old Man that he was concerned because when he sold the maroon Cadillac for Bill, he gave Bill cash, which could mean more trouble with the IRS for not reporting the income.

The Old Man avoided addressing this directly at first, and talked about the time my dad visited him in Tucson, emphasizing that Dad's visit was purely social.

"We didn't discuss anything," Dad agreed. "We're just friends."

"That's right," the Old Man replied.

"The wife was there...We talked about history, dinner, nothing... The thing that I was concerned about was what happened on that transaction with Bill. Supposin' that—"

"Don't mention the boy's name."

"Okay, all right. The tall one. I understand...What should I do now if they give me a subpoena for the records?"

"The records?"

"Yes."

"Do you have records there?"

"Yes."

"What do the records say?"

"Well, it shows that around $9,700 in cash was turned over in the sale of a Cadillac...If they should ask me why, I don't know what to say. This is why I wanted to talk to you."

"Yes, right. But I never knew this."

"In the subpoena, in the records, it'll be there that Bill received the money on a Cadillac in cash."

"But can it be taken out or what? Can the records be taken out?"

"Sure."

"That's all. That only plays safe. You'll ruin him," the Old Man said, referring to the fact that Bill would go back to prison.

"Okay, you want me to pull the records then and burn them?" my dad asked.

"Sure. That's right."

"Well, this is why I called. This is new to me, and I needed help," my dad said, reinforcing the fact that he was relying on Bonanno's expertise in this area, which probably boosted the Old Man's ego.

After they talked a little more, Bonanno said, "I gotta go...I appreciate that you called. That thing is very dangerous."

"Well, that's why I called, because it's one car, and I'll do exactly what you want me to do. That will make me part of the family, won't it?"

"Of course," the Old Man said and laughed. "Pull out the paper from the Cadillac and destroy it. Not in your house."

"No, I'll burn...no, I'll just eat it!" They both laughed.

"Okay. So there is nothing there. You did it right," the Old Man said.

With that conversation, my dad knew he had the concrete evidence the FBI had been seeking. As soon as he hung up, my dad went straight to Bob and delivered the tape.

"Should I make a copy?" Bob asked. He only made duplicates if my dad felt the tapes contained useful information.

"Well," Dad said nonchalantly. "There isn't much, but you might as well."

They listened to the tape as it was copied, and Bob suddenly jumped out of his chair and gave my dad a big hug. "You got him!" he shouted. "You got him!"

In the months that followed, the FBI referred to this tape as the Smoking Gun—the conversation that nailed Joe Bonanno Sr.

A couple months later, the Old Man was indicted by the federal grand jury in San Francisco on five counts, including conspiring to obstruct justice. Jack DiFilippi was indicted on seven counts, including obstruction of justice, because he met Dad at his apartment to discuss and help hide the records of Bill's car sale.

After the indictment, the Old Man's attorney received the discovery documents with all of the evidence—including the name of the concerned citizen who had assisted the FBI: a car dealer named Louis E. Peters.

Bob knew the Old Man would use any means necessary to keep my dad from testifying. One FBI report warned that the "possibility of retribution to silence Peters must be considered due to Bonanno Sr.'s propensity for violence." The report was right: in the lead-up to the trial, Bob learned that a Vegas hitman had been hired to kill my dad.

Bob quickly arranged for Dad to enter witness protection in La Jolla, California, where Bob rented a beachfront penthouse apartment so he could hide in style. Bob later told me, "It was expensive for the Bureau, but your dad deserved it."

In early May 1980, Dad flew from Sacramento to San Diego. Bob and another agent were scheduled to pick up Dad at baggage claim and drive him to the penthouse in La Jolla. Bob's one direction to my dad was, "Don't draw attention to yourself."

When Bob and the other agent arrived at baggage claim and didn't see Dad, Bob became concerned. They looked around and spotted a man in traditional Arab clothing—a long robe, sandals, sunglasses, and a checkered keffiyeh held by a black igal. The Arab man turned toward the agents, took off his sunglasses, and burst out laughing. Even with his life in danger, he had time for a joke. That's my dad.

To combat the boredom in witness protection, my dad bought himself a bike and spent hours riding around La Jolla. Despite Dad's protests, the FBI reimbursed him for the bike, which was likely the only one ever purchased by the Bureau, according to Bob.

The Old Man and Jack's trial preliminaries began in the San Jose District Court during the last week in May. When he met with the prosecuting attorney to prepare for the trial and to go over all of the evidence, the lawyer said, "Lou Peters, you're my biggest problem. How the hell am I going to explain you to the judge to convince him of everything you've done for the Bureau? I could walk up and down the streets of America for ten years and never find another Lou Peters."

Dad was surprised at the attorney's comment. In his mind, he was simply doing what needed to be done.

When my dad took the stand, the Old Man's attorney, Albert Krieger—the mob's go-to defense attorney—repeatedly tried to break him over the four days he testified. At one point, he got in my dad's face and yelled, "You lied to Mr. Bonanno, didn't you?"

"Yes, I lied to Mr. Bonanno," my dad said calmly, looking directly at the attorney. "I lied very well. That's why I'm alive today."

After Dad testified, Bob wanted him to return to La Jolla for safety, but he refused. He had been away from us for over two years and wanted to come home.

Knowing a jury wouldn't side with Bonanno, Albert Krieger requested a trial by judge, which Judge William Ingram granted. While waiting for a verdict, Dad worried that perhaps the judge was in the Mafia's pocket and could be bought.

On September 2, 1980, Honorable Judge Ingram handed down his decision. He found the Old Man and Jack DiFilippi guilty of conspiring to obstruct justice and said, "The evidence and testimony of Louis Peters left no doubt to the guilt of both Joe Bonanno Sr. and Jack DiFilippi." It was the Old Man's first felony conviction in a sixty-year life of crime.

Dad was happy about the conviction but wished he would have had more time to get the Old Man on something heavier than obstruction of justice. As he told the FBI in a later interview, Bonanno "is seventy-four, seventy-five, but he is also a killer. And for the hurt he created for people across the country, he doesn't deserve sympathy. He doesn't deserve anything but the punishment that the law requires based on the conviction he has received."

In that same interview, Dad also reflected on his work with Bob Anderson and the other FBI agents, as well as the example he hoped to set for other businessmen who might be faced with a similar dilemma:

> They are very sincere, caring about me as an individual. I would come up with some really wild ideas because I wanted to nail the Bonannos. They were always very protective of me, making sure that my safety was always number one on their list.

> Agents I met were pleased to work with me because I was trying to do something that they had been trying to get businessmen to do all over the United States. And there's a time, I believe, when you have to stand up and be counted for. I agree that I

probably went to the extreme, but that's my way of life. When I tackle something, I believe in going at it 100 hundred percent.

I wanted to go public [with my involvement in this operation] for one reason...I would hope that businessmen across the country would stand up and be accounted for. And if these animals came to their town, that they would at least call the FBI to let them know they're here. They may be nervous. They may be scared, but not half as nervous or half as scared as if these people actually did get into their community and took control over city hall and took control over the police department. They'd have more problems than they could ever dream existed if they didn't stand up to do what's right.

When I heard the news of the conviction, that they were both found guilty, I felt that all the time and all the waiting and all the effort was certainly worth it.

I was very proud of what I did for my country.

When Dad came home after his testimony, Bob persuaded him to always wear a bulletproof vest. As it turned out, however, the bigger danger lurked within.

Me

I can never mention this to anyone. I don't want to terrorize some-one if they don't know about the Second Coming. And if I tell some-one and they confirm that it's true, I'll never survive. My brain will explode.

Do my parents know? Why didn't they tell me? Why did they even have me, knowing I would be faced with this unbearable choice? Maybe they don't know. But I can never ask them.

God just can't come back to Earth and ask everyone, "Do you want to come with me or stay on Earth?" He just can't. What kind of choice is that? If I say yes, I go with God and float around in heaven, and my life is over. I miss out on being an adult, getting married, having children, grandchildren. If I say no, I stay on Earth, but it will be unrecognizable, destroyed by bombs, natural disasters, and people killing each other. I will be stuck here forever. Do I really want to be left here, alone? No, I don't want that either.

I don't want to die. I'm only thirteen.

I wish I had never been born. Now I spend every day trying to survive. How am I going to do that with no one by my side? Everyone seems to want to go with God except me. No one ever looks frightened. Everyone goes about their everyday life as if the Second Coming isn't going to happen. Why aren't they terrified? I have to get better at hiding my feelings, like the way I hide physically. That will be part of my plan.

I also have to make sure that if I live long enough to have children—but I can't have children! That will mean I have to tell them the truth: "God will come for you soon. You won't be able to grow up or have a family." I could never put my child through this kind of terror. It won't matter. I'm sure I'll be dead, whether I go with God or stay on earth, long before I could have children.

Somehow I have to keep God guessing. I have to stay one step ahead. I have to stay hidden. If God can't find me, he can't ask that question. My work is cut out for me. Hiding from God won't be easy.

From the first time I heard about the Second Coming, some version of this vicious cycle of thoughts played in my mind every night as I tried to fall asleep. I'd lay there shaking and panicked, asking myself questions that had no answers, considering the unimaginable truth that God was coming for me and I was going to die. The night I called for my dad was only one in a long, terrifying succession of sleepless nights. Every morning I woke up, happy to be alive, but those thoughts quickly turned to *Is today the day I die?* Being alive meant one more day of hiding, strategizing, worrying about my family, and trying desperately to survive.

* * *

In the weeks and months that followed my conversation with Lori and Debbie, I changed. I was no longer the imaginative, smart student who had won the math contest in sixth grade. I felt like I was in a fog, mindlessly moving through each day. I had a hard time focusing in class and didn't feel motivated to do my school-work. I also stopped caring about my appearance, showering, or wearing deodorant. What was the point of any of those things if we were all going to die? I pretended to be fine around my family, but fear was always close by, hounding me.

Living in a constant state of anxiety caused me to sweat profusely. At a school dance near the end of the school year, I showed up wearing a light peach-colored sweater with pads under my arms to catch the sweat, but I still had huge wet rings under my arms and kept them at my side all night.

A few years earlier, I had developed a slight stutter. After the event, it became much more pronounced, to the point where I couldn't even say my name when I answered the phone. I had never experienced migraines before that spring day, but after-ward, I started having them once a month. They always started with disrupted vision, and then the pain hit so strongly that I vomited.

I also started acting out in ways I never had before. When a Mexi-can girl at school told me repeatedly that I shouldn't be friends with another Mexican girl, I told her I didn't care what she thought. When she wanted to fight, I agreed, even though I didn't want to be violent.

Though I was scared, I didn't let it show. I agreed to meet the girl in the side yard of her house and asked Debbie to come with me. At the appointed time after school, as we stood face to face, surrounded by several of her friends and Debbie, I said, "I really don't want to fight you. This is stupid."

She stared at me silently, with a defiant look, while the crowd around us shouted, "No!" "You can't back down." "Hit her! Hit her! Hit her!"

So, I hit her square in the face, hoping it would end there. It didn't. She hit me in the face too, and I followed with a punch to her face and chest and then her face again. I just kept hitting, more to keep her from hitting me than to inflict real damage. As my arms almost robotically punched again and again, I thought, *This doesn't feel normal. This isn't me. Why am I doing this?*

Then the girl fell down. A couple of her friends went to her, while everyone else in the crowd looked at me. I dropped my arms and said, "I'm done. This is over." I looked over at Debbie and said, "Let's go."

I never had another problem with that girl, and I stayed friends with the person we were fighting over. Like my dad, I never cared about someone's race or background. I hated school cliques and made friends with people from many different groups. I had no reason to be in that fight.

Though I continued to hang out with Debbie, I slowly stopped spending time with Lori. I said "hi" in the halls at school, but I kept the conversation short because I was afraid she would start talking to me about the Second Coming. Debbie had so much drama at home that she was less likely to bring it up. I also became friends with people, mainly guys, who weren't likely to make God a topic of discussion.

At some point, Sam and I broke up, although I don't remember making it official. Maybe I had changed so much that he didn't like hanging around me, or maybe we simply drifted apart. I didn't see the point of being girlfriend and boyfriend, since I knew we wouldn't live long enough to get married. Plus, I didn't want to care about someone and then have him give a different answer than me at the Second Coming and be separated forever.

Toward the end of eighth grade, I started hanging out with a boy in my class named Jamie. About two weeks before graduation, during my lack-of-hygiene phase, Jamie and I went to Lodi Lake and kissed for the first time. Then he started to put his hand down the front of my pants. I remembered that I hadn't been taking care of myself and tried to stop him. I thought I stopped him in time—until the next day in class when I heard Jamie tell some classmates how bad I smelled, and that he couldn't wash my scent off his hand.

So embarrassed that my lack of personal hygiene had become public knowledge, I immediately went back to showering and never spent time alone with Jamie again. Still, I couldn't deny that fooling around took my mind off hiding from God, and I began using this effective coping mechanism from then on.

I also started smoking and drinking as a way to escape. There was a catch, though: I couldn't get so drunk that I couldn't react if necessary to hide and save myself. I also couldn't stray too far from home because I had to make sure my family and I were together when God broke through the sky and asked the question, if only to tell them how much I loved them before they disappeared.

Though I couldn't wrap my brain around how and when the Second Coming would happen, I desperately tried to. I needed to understand it because I wanted to be ready. I didn't want any more surprises. But the more I tried to figure it out—the more I started picturing God's appearance and a future where I die no matter which way I answer—the more unreal the outside world seemed, like a movie set that would collapse if pushed. Looking into the far distance at the seemingly fake trees or clouds or sky caused me to panic.

Even if I wasn't having these strange episodes, I felt exposed and vulnerable anytime I was outside, especially when I was in a flat open area on a cloudless sunny day, like the day Lori and Debbie told me about the Second Coming. Anything in the sky that looked different—a lunar eclipse or lightning on a clear evening— caused my anxiety to spike. It might mean the sky was about to open up in preparation for judgment. I was convinced that if God saw me out there, he would ask me that fucked-up question before anyone else, and I couldn't have that. I needed him to ask my family first, so I could hear their response.

To distract myself from these thoughts and the seemingly unreal world, I looked for ways to focus my attention on other things. If I had to be outside, I developed a plan in each situation to keep myself focused: in softball, I played third base, so I was close to the action, and I chanted, "Hey, batter, batter," until the ball was hit. Tennis was harder, because I was so far away from the person serving the ball on the other side of the net, so I usually played doubles for more up-close action.

In the house, I also found ways to focus up close. I would sit in the center of the bathroom counter between the two sinks and pick at my face in the mirror for forty-five minutes or more. I spent hours at a time listening to music on my eight-track player. I discovered masturbation as another effective way to keep my mind occupied for hours at a time.

I also relied heavily on our family's planned events, like birthday parties, vacations, and Dad's work projects. Having something on the calendar kept me grounded and somehow assured me that God wasn't coming back yet because we had this or that planned. Over the next few years, I actually became addicted to having events on the calendar. If we didn't have something scheduled—more specifically, if my dad didn't have a work event or trip scheduled—I could easily slip into a panic attack. In my mind, if Dad was working on a project, taking a trip, or attending an upcoming party, God would hold off. Dad was very important, and God wouldn't dare piss him off like that. Without something planned, however, God could come at any time. Dad's presence in my life, even if he was on a trip and not literally in the house, kept me hopeful and sane.

* * *

"I saw you outside the house today, wearing your bathing suit top," my grandmother said from the other twin bed. My mom's mother was visiting from Maine and was staying in my room. A few friends had stopped by earlier that day, and I was hanging out with them on the landing outside our front door, wearing my bikini top and blue jean cut-offs.

"It's hot outside, Grammy," I replied. "And we were thinking about going swimming."

"You do not dress like that outside!"

"But Grammy—"

"No! That is not the way a young lady dresses outside, especially with boys. You look like a whore!"

"No, I don't, Grammy."

"Yes, you do. You're a whore!"

I was stunned into silence, but my sister Les wasn't. She slept in the room next to mine and must have heard my grandmother's rant. I heard my bedroom door open, and there was Les in the doorway. She yelled, "Don't you talk to my sister like that! Leave her alone. Lori, come sleep with me in my room."

I got out of bed and followed Les out the door. I was in awe. Les standing up to Grammy? That certainly took my mind off of being killed by God.

The next morning when I walked into the kitchen, my grand-mother walked toward me and put her arms around me. I cringed, wanting so badly to push her away. Instead, I stood there with my arms plastered to my sides, waiting for her to let go.

"I'm sorry, Lori," my grandmother said. "I shouldn't have said those things."

I didn't believe her, and I didn't respond. I just wanted her to go back to Maine, to the simple backwoods God-fearing town of Washburn. *If you come back today, God, by all means, take my grandmother. And if everyone else who goes with you is like her, I'm definitely going to take my chances here on Earth.*

My grandmother's words got to me. I thought of the time when I didn't wear a bra to Sam's house, despite my mother's recommendation, and then came close to being kidnapped. I felt so guilty for not listening to my mom, like I had caused that man to grab my sweater because I wasn't wearing a bra. *Am I a whore for wearing my bikini top out front?* I wondered. *Am I a bad person for experimenting with Sam and Jamie?* My mom certainly didn't think I should be letting boys touch me, but I liked the way it made me feel.

Lori and Debbie made it sound like I should want to go with God and that saying no to God would be a bad decision, one I could never take back. But I *wanted* to say no. Did wanting to say no to God make me a bad person?

Not long after I started ninth grade, a senior named Curtis invited me to a school dance, and of course I said yes. He was a senior, after all! When he picked me up, we drove to a burger place and talked, and never made it to the dance. We started dating, and soon after, he wanted to have sex. I was a virgin and scared, but Curtis told me that even though it would hurt at first, the pain would go away. He talked me through, and after a few minutes, it was over.

Though I didn't experience orgasm that time or any other time Curtis and I had sex, I enjoyed the distraction of being close to someone. My experience confirmed what I found with Sam and Jamie: hugging, kissing, touching, and being touched was an effective way to keep my mind off dying.

A month after Curtis and I started dating, his younger brother Bryan asked me to type up a report for him. I said yes, excited to show off my skills. Typing required up-close focus, and I loved the distraction it provided.

After I typed the report, I called Bryan, and we set up a time to meet at his house. When I arrived, Bryan answered the door and led me down the hall to his bedroom. I was so proud of what I had typed and couldn't wait to show him. Once inside, I handed him the folder with his report, waiting in anticipation for his response, but he didn't even look at it. He set it down on the dresser and then walked over to the side of his bed and sat down facing the doorway.

"Come over and have a seat," he said.

"Why?" I asked.

"I just want to talk with you and see how things are going."

I sat down, and after a few minutes, Bryan got up and walked over to the doorway. I thought he was leaving the room to get something, but instead, he shut the door.

"What are your parents going to think with the bedroom door shut?"

"My parents aren't home. No one is home."

I was confused. *He knows Curtis is my boyfriend,* I thought, just as he sat down and leaned in to kiss me. Then he pushed me down on the bed and put one hand on the waist of my pants.

"What are you doing?" I asked, struggling to move his hand. "I'm dating your brother."

"It's okay!" he said.

"No! I don't want to do this." I tried to sit up, but he held me down and unzipped his pants.

"Don't worry. You'll like it."

I knew I didn't have a chance against a tall, muscular football player, so I zoned out.

When he was done, Bryan stood up and zipped his pants. "You need to leave. My mom will be home soon."

I pulled up my pants, feeling sick and dirty, and then let myself out. I walked home in a daze, mind racing. *I shouldn't have gone into his bedroom. Why did I follow him? I felt safe to do so. But I still shouldn't have. This wouldn't have happened if I didn't follow him.* I started to cry.

Based on my experience in the school counselor's office, I knew my mom thought I was too young to be fooling around with guys, and this contributed to my sense that doing so made me a bad person. To me, being raped simply confirmed my badness. *Why would anyone care if a bad person like me was raped?* With that thought, I knew I couldn't tell my mom what happened, or anyone else for that matter. I just had to put it behind me. I had to forget it happened. *Keep your focus on staying alive, Lori. God is coming soon.*

* * *

Living on high alert does have its advantages, as I discovered during my sophomore year. One night, my nine-year-old sister Lisa and I were home alone when the power went out. We lit candles and entertained ourselves until the lights came on about thirty minutes later. We cheered and danced. I showed Lisa how to blow out the flame just like mom.

"Put your hand in front of your mouth like this," I said, putting my hand open and fingers separated, palm toward my mouth. "Then carefully blow through your fingers." Lisa nodded, and we skipped around the house, blowing out candles.

From the bedroom, I suddenly heard Lisa scream and then yell, "Lori, Lori, hurry!"

I ran back to the family room to find Lisa screaming, crying, and covering her left eye. I led her to the kitchen and told her, "I'm going to rinse your eye out with water."

I turned on the faucet and then picked her up with one arm and leaned her against the counter with her head over the sink. Then I cupped my other hand under the running water.

"Okay, Lisa, get ready. Now! Open your eye!"

I put my hand with the water against her eye as she screamed and opened it. "Okay, open and close your eye...Open and close your eye...Let me get more water...Okay, Lisa, ready. Open your eye... close it. Open, close."

Finally I put her down. Her screaming stopped. "How does it feel now?"

"It still hurts," she said through her tears.

"Okay, come with me."

I took her hand and led her to our new eye doctor neighbor who lived two houses away. *Please be home, please be home,* I thought as I knocked on the door. The doctor himself opened it a few seconds later. I explained who we were and what had happened and how I had washed out her eye with cold water.

"Come on in," he said and led us to the couch in the family room. "I'll be right back."

A few minutes later, he returned with a doctor's bag and asked Lisa to lie down on the couch, with her head under a big lamp that sat on an end table. He put on a pair of gloves and opened her eyes, asking her to look up and down and side to side.

"She has wax in her eye, and it has hardened," the doctor explained to me. "I will remove as much as I can, but she will need to follow up with an eye doctor because I don't have all of my equipment at home."

I told him I understood.

"You probably saved your sister's eye. The best thing you could have done was harden the wax with cold water so it didn't burn her eye anymore."

I was so grateful I hadn't made her eye worse.

After he finished, he put some drops in Lisa's eye and gave me his card. "Have your parents call me if they have any questions." We thanked him and then walked home. I felt so proud of myself. I realized I was capable in an emergency, even through all my fear.

* * *

During my junior year, I dated a couple of high school guys, but found that I needed someone older, someone more mature—someone who could challenge me and also help me survive if all hell broke loose at the Second Coming. One day at Lodi Lake, I met just the guy.

Bob was around six years older than me, handsome and smart. He had layered, dark wavy hair, brown eyes, and a gorgeous smile. He was also going through a divorce, but that didn't matter to me. What mattered was his knowledge, strength, and ability to protect me and keep me safe. During sex, he was loving, gentle, and romantic, always lighting candles to set the mood.

With Bob, I learned more about what guys like. I tried oral sex for the first time and realized I enjoyed it because I could narrow my focus to one very specific activity. And with Bob's help and even tips from my sister Les, I became good at it, which gave me a sense of value in knowing I could bring pleasure to a guy.

The summer before my senior year, Bob and I drove into the foothills in his 1960s cargo van. We brought along Bob's dog, Genghis Khan, and spent the day playing with Genghis, eating, talking, kissing, and drinking. At the end of the day, we packed up and headed down the bumpy gravel road.

On the way, Genghis tried to wedge his way between the two front seats for some attention, but there wasn't room for all three of us.

"I'll just go sit with him," I told Bob and crawled to the back.

The cargo van didn't have any bench seats, so I squatted and balanced on my feet with my back facing the side double doors. As I tried to settle Genghis, Bob hit a big pothole. The van bounced, causing me to lose my balance and fall against the doors, which flew open, and out I went.

Don't hit your head! I told myself. Ever since I felt my brain shift, I was convinced something was wrong with my head, and I was terrified of making it worse. As I fell, I turned my body so I landed hard on my left hip and then rolled down the road. I tried to stop myself with my hands, but I was rolling too fast. *Stop. Stop. Stop.* I kept telling myself, until finally I did.

I laid there for a second, wondering if Bob noticed I was gone. I lifted my head and watched the van move farther away and then suddenly brake. I lowered my head, closed my eyes, and waited.

"Are you okay?" Bob asked, leaning over me. "I swear I locked those side doors! Let's go down to the creek and clean you up."

He helped me stand and then led me toward the creek, one painful step at a time. Because of the deep road burn on my left hip, I couldn't put any weight on that foot, and I leaned heavily on Bob. At the creek, Bob tried to wash the wounds under my shredded pants and shirt, but the pain was excruciating. He helped me back to the van, and we drove back to his parents' house, where he had been living after separating from his wife. He helped me inside and onto the couch, covered me with a blanket, and then called my mom. When she arrived, Mom took one look at me—disheveled, anxious, and clearly in pain—and said, "I'm taking her to the hospital."

"Oh, I think she's okay," Bob said, and his mom agreed. "She just needs some rest."

"No," my mom said. "I'm taking her to the hospital. She needs to be looked at."

At the emergency room, we learned I had a slight concussion and a deep hip contusion. The doctor told me I was really lucky. "If you would have fallen forward instead of backward, you would have seen what was happening and instinctively stiffened. Most likely, you would have broken your neck."

The most painful part was having the nurses clean out my road burns. It felt like something straight out of a torture scene from a horror movie. They scrubbed and scrubbed until there was not one speck of gravel left. Although the cleaning process hurt like hell, having people near me, helping me, caused me to feel safe, and my anxiety subsided.

My parents knew I was dating Bob, but they didn't know he was married—until I decided to "help" my boyfriend by telling my dad that Bob was having trouble finding a lawyer for his divorce. On one of the few occasions that Bob came over to my house, my dad happened to be home. He walked into the living room where Bob and I were sitting on the couch, and pulled up a chair like he was going to settle in for a long conversation.

After the initial introductions, Dad said, "So, Bob, I hear you're looking for an attorney."

I got off the couch and sat on the floor between my hero and my strong boyfriend, excited to see how Dad was going to help Bob and how impressed Bob was going to be with Dad's knowledge.

"Yeah, I, uh, I...I'm married," Bob said, flustered, "and I'm thinking I want to get a divorce."

"Oh, well, I can help you with that," my dad said. "Actually, I can get an attorney on the phone right now, and we can get an appointment set up for you."

"Well, uh, I've been looking into some, but I'll keep that in mind."

"Well, you be sure and let me know if you need any help. I'm going to keep track of this, and I'll help you in any way possible." My dad then stood, indicating the conversation was over, and I think Bob took the hint that it was time to leave—and leave me.

After Bob left, my dad turned to me. "You know, honey, I don't think he's serious about getting a divorce."

"Really? But he said he wanted to."

"I know, but some guys are like that. They say they are getting a divorce, but they don't go through with it. Do you think he's the best guy for you?"

My dad knew what he was talking about. Bob moved back in with his wife, and I had a hard time letting go. I would drive by their home after dark, beeping my horn all the way down the street. Bob was everything I felt I needed, and I desperately tried to keep him in my life by reaching out to his friend Brian, another strong, older guy who was well versed in karate just like Bob. By dating Brian, I figured I was bound to run into Bob sometime. The longer Brian and I dated, however, the more my feelings for him grew, and my need for Bob disappeared.

* * *

When I was fifteen, I decided to add marijuana to my list of ways to escape. Big mistake. Shortly after taking a few hits, my anxiety spiked, and I spun out into a full-blown panic attack. Everyone else was stoned, chilling, and satisfying their munchies, but I couldn't stop shaking. After I puked in the kitchen sink, my friend led me to a high-back chair in a corner.

"The effects will go away soon," my friend assured me, while trying to keep the panic out of her own voice. She had never seen me like this, though it certainly wasn't the first time I had panicked to this extreme. "Just try to sleep for a while before you go home."

I drew my knees up to my chest and wrapped my arms around my shins. *This is the pot,* I told myself. *It will go away. Just try to relax. You're at your friend's house. This will go away.* I leaned my head back and closed my eyes, waiting for my thoughts to calm and my panic to subside.

My friend was right. After about an hour, I felt better and walked home, but I also told myself, *You can never do that again. You have to stay alert to stay alive.*

A year later, however, I inadvertently put myself in the same position when I had a cavity filled and the dentist offered a new "laughing gas" in addition to the usual Novocain. Soon after the dentist had me inhale the gas, I did not feel like laughing. I felt agitated and panicky, just like I did after smoking pot—just like I did when I thought too much about the future and the world took on an unreal feeling. I started shaking while the dentist worked on my tooth.

"What's wrong?" he asked.

"This is making me feel awful," I replied.

"The effects will go away in a few seconds," he assured me.

They didn't. After I got home, I laid down on the couch and started shaking uncontrollably.

"Mom!" I yelled.

"What's wrong?" she asked as she walked in.

"I don't know. I don't feel well. I feel like I did when I was at the dentist. Do, uh, do you think some of the gas is still inside me?" I asked, hoping that was the case but fearing it was related to the brain shift. Thinking about my broken brain made me panic even more.

Because I had become so skilled at hiding my inner terror, my mom had never seen me like this. She called the dentist's office and described my condition so convincingly that the dentist came by the house on his way home.

"The gas is very safe," he told my mother. "I can assure you that all of the effects are gone. With the state she's in, I recommend taking her to a psychologist."

I knew it! I thought, frantic. *Something is wrong with my brain! I'm going to have these attacks forever, and I'm going to die. When will this end? I don't want to die. I want to feel normal.*

About a month later, my parents drove me to my first appointment with the psychologist. When Dad turned onto the highway, I started panicking. There were plenty of doctors in Lodi. *Why are we getting on the highway? Where are they really taking me?* If Mom and Dad were doing this together, and if Dad was missing work for this appointment, it must be serious.

"Are you taking me to a nuthouse and leaving me there?" I finally asked from the back seat.

"No, we're not leaving you at a hospital," my dad said.

I didn't quite believe them and thought my suspicions were confirmed when we pulled into the driveway of a tall old building surrounded by giant trees that appeared to block any light from entering the tiny windows. It looked like an insane asylum straight out of the movies. Thankfully, we drove past the "asylum" toward a one-story building that resembled a regular office building.

Inside, we met the psychologist, who asked me to wait in her office while she talked to my parents. I breathed a little easier when I saw that her office had a normal desk and chairs and was not a padded room.

After a few minutes, the counselor walked in and said, "Your parents told me you were really scared and anxious recently, and I would like to talk to you to find out why you think that might be happening."

I knew I couldn't tell her the real reason because I couldn't risk having her confirm the truth, so I said, "I don't know. Sometimes I just get really scared, and I start shaking."

She asked more questions, and I answered somewhat honestly. Toward the end, she said, "Well, we can try something called biofeedback to help you relax. Then when you're feeling anxious and shaky, you can talk yourself into relaxing."

"Oh, okay. That sounds good," I said, but I didn't see the point. Being able to calm myself down would be nice, but it didn't fix the problem: God was still coming back, and I was going to die, either immediately or in the near future when the earth and everything in it were destroyed.

* * *

Since marijuana wasn't a possible escape route and therapy had nothing to offer me, I stuck to alcohol. One night, Les took me with her to the "White House," a two-story dilapidated rental used as a party house in a rural part of Lodi. While Les went off to find Omar, her on-again, off-again boyfriend, I had a few drinks and engaged in limited conversation with a couple of stoned partiers.

I walked outside and strolled around the property, reflecting on my life and how it had completely changed since I learned about the Second Coming. As I thought about the constant battle against fear, panic attacks, and "fake world" episodes, my anger and frustration grew. Finally, it built to the point where I felt bold enough to look up into the starry sky, throw my arms out wide, and scream, "God, I'm right here! I'm right here! Come and get me, you son of a bitch!"

I waited a minute, staring up at the sky. Nothing happened. I lowered my arms, somewhat relieved. I walked back into the house and looked around at the partiers lounging around the disheveled house, many too stoned or drunk to stay awake or hold a conversation. When the Second Coming happened, they would be completely unaware and unprepared. *This is not how I want to live the time I have left*, I thought. I never returned to the White House again.

On another weekend, when I was seventeen, I drove to the Clements Stampede with two friends. It was a hot, dusty day—perfect drinking weather. We took the party into the car and drank a little more on the way back to Lodi as we talked about the handsome cowboys and beautiful horses.

Before we went home, we decided to drive through Lodi Lake. The road wound three-quarters of the way around the lake and then looped back toward the entrance.

Soon after we turned around, a police car pulled us over.

"Oh shit!" I said as I glanced in my rearview mirror. "Why is he pulling me over?"

In the back, Kathy started shoving beer bottles under the seat, and we all tried to look as sober as possible. When the policeman walked up, I opened my door and stepped outside. In my buzzed state, I felt sure that I could keep the officer from looking in the car by chatting him up.

"What are you guys doing today?" the policeman asked, peeking into the car window behind me.

"We just drove back from the Clements Stampede," I said. "We decided to stop by the lake on our way home."

"Do you know that you don't have a license plate on the back of your vehicle?"

"Oh, yes," I said matter of factly. "My license plate was stolen"— which was the truth.

When the officer asked for my insurance information and driver's license, I knew I was in trouble: I had lost my license.

When all was said and done, the officer found the alcohol, and Debbie I were taken to the police station in handcuffs—me because I was drinking and driving without a license plate or driver's license, and Debbie because she didn't have her license either. Kathy did, so she was taken home.

At the station, the officer put Debbie and me in separate rooms for questioning. Debbie was ultimately let go with a warning, and I was released with a court date. My dad wasn't happy about getting that call from the police station; perhaps he even flashed back to his own time in handcuffs as a teenager.

When I appeared in court, the judge dropped the open container charge, and I ended up with a misdemeanor for having no license plate and no driver's license while operating a vehicle. My punishment: one day at a work farm. I felt so lucky that it wasn't worse—until my mom drove me to the parking lot by the juvenile detention center, and I saw several teenage male inmates standing next to two buses.

"Mom, I don't want to get out of the car!" I said.

"Well, you have to. I'm sure you won't be going with those boys."

As mom drove off, I took my place in line to step onto one of the buses with a large group of male inmates and one male officer. On the drive to our destination, it became clear that the boys were proud of their status and their criminal record. My companions had committed murder, assault, drug offenses, and robbery.

"Why are you here?" one of the inmates asked.

"I didn't have a license plate and driver's license," I said.

The bus erupted with laughter, and I joined them, trying to connect.

"They put you on this bus with *us* for no license plate?" someone asked, shaking his head and chuckling. As I looked around, the other guys seemed similarly amused that I was here for such a small offense. *Oh boy*, I thought. *This is going to be a long day.*

The bus pulled up to a vacant house on the outskirts of town. After we walked inside, the officer pulled out his clipboard and started asking for volunteers to clean various areas.

"Who wants to work on the bathroom?" he asked.

"I will," I said, thinking I would be in there alone.

"Who wants to clean the bathroom with Lori?" the supervisor asked.

A tall, thin inmate raised his hand. *Oh no,* I thought. Whereas the other boys laughed and talked on the bus, this one had been silent the whole time. He was a complete unknown.

The officer showed us to the bathroom and told us to get to work, closing the door behind him when he left.

I knelt at one end of the tub and started scrubbing. Suddenly, the other inmate knelt beside me and, without a word, reached up with his hand and pushed the hair off my forehead and then stroked the long strands. I immediately stopped scrubbing, keeping my eyes straight ahead, and he quickly lowered his arm. A minute or so later, the inmate started stroking my hair again while breathing heavily.

I froze. *Shit,* I thought. *The door is shut. No one will hear me scream if he tries to beat or rape me.* As he continued caressing my hair, I stared straight ahead at the wall above the tub and said in a soft, even voice, "Please stop doing that."

At once, he took his hand away and didn't touch me again. Though his silence still made me nervous, the fact that he stopped when I asked helped me to view him a little differently. He might still be dangerous, but he also seemed like a loner who was struggling with deep-seated issues just like me.

At the end of the day, the officer whistled and called everyone to the front room, announced that we were done, and told us to board the bus. On the ride back, it became apparent that my attempts to hide my fear had worked. The boys wanted to stay in touch and invited me to come visit them at juvenile hall; one even gave me his phone number because he was getting out the following week.

After we were dropped off, I walked toward my mom's car. Just before I got in, I turned, smiled, and waved to my new friends, glad I would never see them again.

"Did you know that I spent the day with murderers and drug dealers?" I asked my mom as soon as I closed the door. She was visibly shocked, but still made excuses for the organizers, saying it must have been some administrative mix-up. Dad, on the other hand, was livid when he discovered his daughter had been left alone with a male inmate behind a closed door—and he made his feelings known to the powers that be. In turn, the courts changed their procedures when it came to work farm punishment for teenage girls. *My hero!*

Several months later, my counselor set up a group session with several of her patients. I had been seeing the same therapist about twice a month since the day I thought I was being taken to a nuthouse, but this was the first time she suggested a group session.

I was one of the first to arrive. The chairs were arranged in a circle, and I took a seat facing the door. A few more trickled in, and then the door opened, and in walked the inmate from the bathroom. *No way!* I thought, panic rising.

I clammed up right away and didn't say one word for the entire forty-minute session. Afterward, my therapist stopped me and asked what I thought.

"I don't want to be in the group," I said.

"Oh, why?"

"Well, remember when the judge sent me to work for one day, and I ended up in the bathroom with the inmate who stroked my hair? Well, he was in the group today."

She was shocked and assured me that I didn't have to attend the group. I thanked her and left, and never saw her again. I didn't want to chance running into that guy again.

* * *

When I was sixteen and Les was nineteen, my dad added Fiat to the line of cars sold at the dealership, and he let both of us pick out our very own. Les chose the Fiat X19, and I chose the Fiat Spider. Though I had never driven a five-speed, I gladly embraced the focus required to learn this new skill.

A few months later, the hospital called to tell me that Les had been in a car accident.

Les and Omar were driving back from Omar's family's rural home. Omar was behind the wheel of Les's Fiat, and he drifted off the edge of the road. When he overcorrected, he lost control and crashed into a tree. Omar died instantly, and Les was taken to the emergency room.

"She's in the hospital, but it's nothing serious," the person on the phone said. "She's okay, so don't rush over here."

"Oh, I'm glad she is okay. I promise I won't rush."

On my way to the hospital, I stopped at a red light. After it turned green, I moved into the intersection and glanced down for a second to lower the radio volume. In that instant, a car driving in the opposite direction sped up and turned left in front of me. She hit the front of the driver's side, sending my car to the right corner of the intersection, where it hit a street light post and stopped partially on the sidewalk. The top of my head hit the windshield, and my left knee slammed into the steering column.

After the ambulance took me to the emergency room, my dad's friend and Lodi police chief Marc Yates came in to see me.

"Hi, Lori. How are you feeling?"

"I'm okay."

"How can I reach your parents? Do you know where Lisa is?"

I felt sluggish and couldn't think straight. It took me a few seconds to answer him.

"Um, Lisa is at a sleepover at a friend's house," I said slowly. "Mom and Dad are flying to Switzerland. He won another trip." I paused and then remembered, "Oh, there's a note on the refrigerator with all the information."

"Okay, I'll get in touch with your parents and Lisa. You just get better."

"How's Les?"

"She's doing well. She just left the ER, and she's in her own room. Don't worry. Just rest."

While they were still in flight, my parents received a note from the cockpit that read, "Two of your girls in car accidents. In hospital. One ICU." When they landed, Mom and Dad immediately caught a plane back to San Francisco. Marc Yates had a police vehicle waiting to drive my parents to the hospital in Lodi in record time.

The next morning, the door to my room opened. In my groggy state, I didn't realize at first that it was a man of God—black suit, white collar, sickening smile. "Why are you here?" I blurted out, terrified once I realized what I was seeing. *Am I dying? I can't be dying!*

The man stopped. "I work at the hospital," he replied. "I wanted to know if you would like to—"

"No! I don't want you here. I want you to leave."

"Sorry to bother you," the minister said and left.

I was still shaking when the door opened again, but this time it was my parents. Despite my concussion and broken kneecap, I must have looked good compared to my sister, because my parents' frantic expression turned to relief when they saw me.

"Is Les still in the hospital?" I asked.

"Yes," my mom said.

"I want to see her. Please take me to her."

My parents looked at each other. I could sense hesitation. Finally, my mom spoke. "Les had to have surgery. She has bruises, and she isn't awake yet."

Though my mom tried to warn me, nothing could have prepared me for what I saw.

Dad wheeled me down the hall to ICU, and Mom walked next to me. After we entered the room, I looked around and asked, "Where's Les?"

"She's right there," my dad said, nodding toward the person in the bed before me, unrecognizable due to her swollen face and arms, bruised skin, bandages, casts, traction wires, and third-degree burns from a cigarette she was smoking.

"No, that can't be my sister," I said, tears in my eyes. I had never seen anything so brutal.

"No, Lori. That is Les. She's just swollen," my mom said.

Les's accident was clearly more serious than I had been told. I began to panic. A fog descended over my brain, and I started shaking uncontrollably.

"Please take me back to my room," I cried. My mom turned my wheelchair and pushed me out of the room as I thought, *My sister is dying. God, don't kill my sister. Don't punish her. I'm the bad one. I'm the one who doesn't want to go with you.*

The doctors gave Les a fifty-fifty chance of surviving. She did survive, but she was never the same. Omar's death devastated her, and the accident itself damaged part of her brain. She started doing heavy drugs and refused to wear a seatbelt while driving, despite the fact that Omar wasn't wearing one when he died.

After my accident and seeing Les in the ICU, I always wore my seatbelt, and I asked her once, "Les, why don't you wear a seatbelt?"

"When it's your time to die, it doesn't matter if you have a seatbelt on or not," she said simply.

"Well, you don't have to push it!" I shot back. She looked at me and smiled as if to say, "Well done, Sis." I smiled to myself. That was one of the few times I outdid her.

Nearly twenty years after Omar's death, Les was in another, very similar accident. It was the day before her husband Jim's birthday in 1994. She was driving alone on a rural road when she drifted off the road, overcorrected, and hit a utility pole. Les wasn't wearing a seatbelt and flew through the windshield. She died in the ER.

I spoke at Les's memorial service and shared how much my sister meant to me. Aside from my dad, Les was the family member I could count on for advice and support. She answered questions about my body and sex that no one else would. Les struggled after the accident in which Omar died, but I needed the people present at her intimate service to remember her amazing qualities: her creativity, the fact that she wrote poetry and sewed many of her own clothes, her fearlessness, her take-no-prisoners confidence.

At that point in my life, I was having trouble focusing on everyday tasks. But as I talked about Les, I didn't miss a single word, I didn't lose my place, and I didn't shed a tear, empowered by my big sister's inner strength.

* * *

In 1975, Dad had two heart attacks. After the second one, his doctor gave him some strong advice: change the way you eat or start exercising. Dad loved his steak and lobster and told me, "No one is going to tell me what to eat. I will eat what I want to eat." So, exercise it was.

One spring morning, Dad decided to go for a walk around our suburban neighborhood.

"Dad, why are you dressed like you're hiking the Appalachian trail?" I asked with a laugh as he headed for the front door.

In typical Dad fashion, his walking attire was over the top: a white V-neck T-shirt, blue-and-white-striped knee-length shorts, calf-height wool socks, heavy-duty hiking boots, a red bandana folded and tied around his forehead, all topped off by a five-foot-tall, three-inch-diameter heavy wood walking stick.

"My doctor told me I had to walk for my health," he said mischievously.

I laughed and thought, *Yeah, but I doubt he said to dress like that!*

One summer day, not long after that morning, my friend Debbie's ring came off in our pool and got stuck in the drain at the deep end. We both tried to pull it out but had no luck. I knew Dad would know what to do, so I went into the house and explained what happened. He walked out to the pool with me and surveyed the situation.

"Wait right here," he told us, then disappeared into the house.

"This is going to be good," I told Debbie. "Just wait." As it turned out, we weren't disappointed.

A few minutes later, the screen door opened, and out walked Dad looking like a SCUBA class dropout. He was wearing swim trunks, goggles, and a snorkel, and he had a brick that was criss-cross tied with rope sitting horizontally against his stomach, held in place by the rope wrapped around his waist. He held pliers and a screwdriver in one hand and asked me to get him the garden hose, which he held in the other. He then strolled to the deep end of the pool, a man on a mission. He stepped on the diving board and walked to the edge hanging over the water.

"Dad, what are you doing?" I asked, unable to stop laughing.

"You want me to get the ring, don't you?" he asked playfully. Debbie and I just nodded and laughed.

"Wait! Don't jump in! I have to take a picture." I ran into the house to get my camera and captured Dad MacGyver for posterity.

"Okay, turn on the hose," Dad said. After I did so, he jumped in, sank to the bottom, and in less than two minutes, rose to the surface, his right hand lifted high out of the water holding the ring. Debbie and I cheered.

I loved my dad's sense of humor. I loved his unique personality. Through everyday incidents like these, he played a monumental part in saving me. He didn't know it, and I couldn't have articulated it at the time, but in making me laugh and keeping life interesting at home, he kept me sane, grounded, and secure. Around my dad, I felt as safe as I could be against the imminent Second Coming.

I couldn't imagine life without him.

* * *

In October of my senior year, on a relatively quiet evening, my dad said, "Lori, let's go for a drive."

After we drove around and chit-chatted for a bit, he said, "I want to tell you something."

"Okay."

"Your mom and I are getting legally separated. I have—"

"What? No, no, no! That can't happen. You can't do that! You just can't!"

"Lori, wait a minute, wait a minute—"

"How could you do that to Mom? No, no, no. That can't happen!"

The issue wasn't really Mom. I was panicked at the thought of him not living at home. I shook my head from side to side and shifted around in my seat. If he moved out, how would I know where to find him when God came back? How would I know his answer to the question? Plus, my safety net would be gone. God could come at any moment, and that would be it. I could be separated from my dad forever. That couldn't happen. It just couldn't.

"Dad, take me home. Take me home. I don't feel good. I gotta go home. I gotta go home."

"Lori, wait—"

"Dad, stop the car! Stop the car!"

Dad pulled over to the curb. As soon as he parked, I opened the door and bolted down the street.

"Lori!"

Dad got out of the car and started chasing me. "Lori, come back. Let me explain."

I stopped and paused for a second to catch my breath. Then I turned around and walked right past him back to the car. He followed. After sliding behind the steering wheel, he turned toward me. "Lori, there's a reason for this. I need to talk to you about it."

I shook my head and stared out the window, fighting back tears.

"We're going to get back together," Dad continued. "This isn't going to last forever. We're going to get back together."

"What do you mean?"

"Your mother and I need to be legally separated so I can sign documents without her signature. I'm working on a very important business project, and I need to be able to do this alone. That's all it is."

"Really? So, you're going to get back together?"

"Yes."

"Well, how long is it going to take?

"I'm not sure exactly, maybe six months to a year."

I considered his words. As terrified as I was at the thought of him not living at home, I believed him. "Okay, so you're just doing this so you can sign papers alone," I said.

"Yes."

"And it's only temporary. You're going to get back together."

"Yes."

"Okay." The panic was still there, bubbling under the surface, but at least I knew he was coming back.

"Are you okay?"

"Yeah, Dad. I'm feeling better knowing you're going to get back together."

We drove back home, and I went straight to my room. I had to think this through, strategize how I was going to survive while he was gone. A big work project meant there would be deadlines and events, which meant God wouldn't come back, not while Dad had so many things going on—which meant I would still be alive. It would be just like when he and mom took a trip: Dad wouldn't be home every night, but he would come back. It wouldn't be forever. I could do this.

My sisters and I never talked about the separation, and I never talked about it with my mom either—another one of those secrets we lived with but didn't discuss. Though I wanted to believe my dad's reason for the separation, I was a little skeptical. I worked part time at my dad's dealership, and he signed checks and other documents all the time without my mom's signature. Still, I trusted him completely that it was temporary and that he would come back home as soon as he could.

* * *

When I graduated from high school in June 1978, there was Dad, sitting alone in the stands, probably fresh off the trip to Miami where he met with the financier and got separated from Bob Anderson at the airport. To keep up appearances, he didn't sit with my mom, but he still wanted to support me. As I learned later, he wasn't by himself; FBI agents also sat in the stadium, keeping an eye on him.

After the ceremony, my mom and dad both joined me on the field. My mom took a photo of my dad and me, and my dad took a photo of my mom and me. When I look at the two photos, I see and feel the differences in my relationship with each of my parents. With my dad, I'm smiling and leaning my head on his shoulder, and he has his arm around me. I'm clearly at ease and relaxed, comfortable and secure in his presence. My smile says, "I made it, I actually graduated, despite major anxiety and panic!" In the photo with my mom, we're both smiling and my arm is around her shoulders, but we appear more formal and posed.

After high school, I enrolled in a few classes at the community college in Stockton, but I struggled to keep up. In high school, concentrating in class had become increasingly difficult, even in subjects like math, which I loved. More than once during high school, my anxiety reached a point where I asked my dad to call the school to change my class schedule because I couldn't focus long enough to write a term paper or understand the math concepts. The same problems carried over into college.

In addition, the sense that the outside world was fake started happening more often, sometimes soon after I walked out the front door. After my dad moved, there were days when the feeling was so strong that I couldn't leave the house. Other days I would be okay until I reached the large stretch of open farmland on my twenty-five-minute drive to the community college. Suddenly, the world outside would shift and appear unreal. My fight-or-flight response would kick in, and I would flee back to the safety of my house. The episodes started occurring more frequently and more quickly after leaving my house, so finally, I just stopped going to class.

While the community college was in a different city, the new Mervyn's department store was only ten minutes from my house, and I didn't need to drive through open stretches to get there. The shorter drive made me feel safe, knowing I could get home quickly if I started to panic, so I took a job there the year after I graduated from high school.

One Friday, my dad came into the store and found me in the children's clothing section. I was so happy to see him, but I was a little surprised. After we talked for a few minutes, I asked, "So, what are you doing here?"

"Well, what are your plans for tonight?"

"I'll probably stay home. Brian will be out with his friends."

"How about I take you out on a date?

"Really? That would be great."

"Okay, I'll pick you up at six."

After work, I drove home and dressed for my "date," excited to have some time with my dad. When he arrived at the house, he actually rang the doorbell, just like a real date would. When I answered, he reached across the threshold and handed me a bouquet of flowers.

"Oh, Dad. Thank you! They're so nice," I said. Inside I smiled, thinking, *You are playing this to the hilt!*

As always, Dad was impeccably dressed. We walked out to his Cadillac, and he opened the door for me. We drove to Black Angus Steakhouse, of course, and Dad decided on steak and lobster, and so did I. He ordered a bourbon and water for himself, and I had a Diet Coke.

As I sat there—talking, laughing, and enjoying my meal with Dad—I thought, *I wonder if anyone thinks we're on an actual date? I wouldn't care if they did!* I felt so special and loved.

At some point, the DJ started playing music, and after we ate, my dad said, "Let's go dance!"

We ended up next to a couple doing choreographed moves, and the guy kept twirling his date right into us. The dance floor was too crowded for the type of dancing they were doing. Finally, my dad said, "Okay, I've had enough of this. Come here, Lori." And he started twirling me right back into them! As the couple moved away from us, the guy glared at my dad, who returned his stare with a look that said, "Don't even think about it."

After we danced to a couple songs, my dad said, "I'm going to take a break. You keep dancing. I'll be up there on the balcony so I can see you having fun."

I walked over and asked a guy to dance, and my dad headed upstairs. While I danced, I looked up and waved at my dad, who waved back and then continued talking to a man I didn't recognize. At the time, I thought it was a customer from the car dealership. We lived in a small town, and people recognized him all the time. I now know he was talking to an FBI agent who had been assigned to watch him for the evening.

Dad taking me on a date meant the world to me. He managed to give me a slice of normalcy, even when he was engaged in something that was anything but normal. Within the next year, I was able to give back a tiny portion of the stability he gave me.

My Dad and Me

During Joe Bonanno Sr.'s trial, my dad suffered intense headaches and blurred vision. The FBI arranged for him to see a doctor, who felt both were related to the stress of giving his testimony. After he returned home, however, my dad experienced more serious symptoms. One time, just as I walked out of my bedroom, I saw Dad walking down the hall toward the kitchen. His body suddenly slammed against the wall and slid down to the floor.

"Dad, are you okay?" I asked, hurrying up to him.

"Oh, yeah, I just tripped," he said. "Can you help me up?"

My dad didn't trip like that, or ask for help, so I thought the whole situation was strange, but I tried to go along as he played it off as no big deal.

A couple weeks later, the doorbell rang. When my fourteen-year-old sister Lisa answered the door, she found Dad lying face-up on the porch with his feet at the door and his head toward the street.

"Hey, Dad," Lisa said. "What are you doing out here?"

"Oh, just looking at the sky," he replied, trying not to alarm her. "Want to give me a hand?"

Lisa helped him up, and then he walked into the house on his own, but in the entryway, he collapsed with a seizure.

"Mom!" Lisa yelled. "Mom!"

After my mom rushed in, she knelt by Dad's side, and then asked Lisa to stay with him while she called 911. Lisa and my mom made him as comfortable as possible on the floor while waiting for the paramedics, then Mom followed the ambulance to Lodi Community Hospital. Dad received an MRI on his brain, and after the doctor viewed the results, he arranged for my dad to be transferred by ambulance to a more equipped facility: St. Joseph's Hospital in Stockton.

Late that afternoon, my sisters and I were summoned to St. Joseph's. Unlike when Dad told each of us individually about our parents' separation, this time, my parents wanted all three of us to drive over together. I wondered what might be wrong, but true to form for our family, I didn't discuss my thoughts with my sisters, and if they were concerned, they didn't say anything either.

When we walked into the hospital room, Dad smiled at us uneasily. His bed had been raised to a sitting position, and Mom stood next to him on the far side of the room. My sisters and I gathered at the foot of the bed, facing my parents. Dad started with, "I have something serious to tell all of you. This is going to be difficult for me to say, and if this becomes too hard for you, I need you to leave the room."

"Okay, Dad," Les and Lisa said together, while I asked, "What's going on? Is something the matter?"

"I've been told I have a large tumor in my brain, and it's cancer. The doctors told me I have six months to live," my dad said slowly, as if he were struggling to hold it together as he spoke.

My sisters and I stood silent at first, in shock. Then I began asking questions: "What do you mean? Are they sure? It must be a mistake."

When I started crying, Mom remained silent and didn't move from her place by the bed. My dad said, "Lori, you need to leave the room and come back after you calm down."

I immediately turned around and hurried out. I knew what I had to do. I walked to the nurses' station and asked if there was a chapel, then followed their directions to the small praying room. I nervously went in and locked the door.

"God," I said, "you know I don't like you. You know I don't want to believe in you. But if you would just let my dad live, I'll stop fighting you. I will do whatever you want. Just save my dad. Please God, don't let my dad die."

I stood there for a few minutes, crying and bargaining. "You son of a bitch, for doing this to my dad," I said finally, and then left the little room, drying my eyes as I walked. When I rejoined my family, everyone stood exactly where they were when I left—my mom at the head of the bed, my sisters at the foot. No one was speaking.

"Well, maybe you guys should just go home," my mom said finally. "I'll be there later."

The three of us kissed and hugged Dad, said our goodbyes, and walked out the door.

The car ride home was eerily silent, partly because we were in shock and partly because we simply didn't talk about these things. *Even now, with Dad dying, we can't bring ourselves to talk,* I thought as I stared out the window from the passenger's seat, while Les drove and Lisa sat quietly in the back seat.

At home, I walked straight to my bedroom and immediately started panicking. With my dad gone forever, I would never be safe. My home, my fortress, would be destroyed. If God could get to Dad, my superhero, I had no chance of survival.

I also knew I couldn't keep the promise I made in the chapel, and I knew God wouldn't keep his end either. Why *would* he help me? He knew I didn't like him. I didn't want to go to heaven. I felt like all of the life incidents that followed my conversation with Lori and Debbie—fooling around with Jamie and other boys, grandmother calling me a whore, the attempted kidnapping, being raped, getting arrested, falling out of a married man's van—confirmed the innate badness revealed in my desire to say no to God. Even if I changed my mind and said yes, I didn't think I deserved to go to heaven, or that God would want me. I felt unworthy.

* * *

When Dad arrived at St. Joseph's Hospital after his seizure, neurosurgeon Dr. Richard Balch reviewed the MRI taken in Lodi and my dad's other symptoms—the headaches, blurred vision, falling—and then ordered a second brain scan with contrast, which revealed what he suspected: grade IV glioblastoma, the most aggressive type of brain cancer. In Dad's case, the tumor had already invaded three of the four lobes on the right side of his brain.

On July 3, 1980, Dad underwent surgery to remove as much of the tumor as possible. By this point, Bob Anderson had married Judy, who worked at St. Joseph's as one of Dr. Balch's surgical nurses and requested to assist during Dad's operation. During surgery, it became clear that the tumor had spread farther into the temporal, parietal, and occipital lobes than the MRI had suggested.

Dad stopped working after surgery and started six weeks of daily radiation. I walked into the kitchen one morning and saw him sitting at the breakfast table, his incision clearly visible on his dry, scaly bald head. The sight of that long, jagged scar and the reality of what it represented made me feel physically sick. As my panic rose, I rushed out the back door into the garage and sobbed. Something about the way he sat there, head bent over his cup of coffee—I just knew he wasn't going to make it. I was devastated.

Given his prognosis, Dad wanted to ensure the separation wouldn't cause legal issues related to the dealership, insurance benefits, and my parents' estate after his death; so on September 27, 1980, my parents renewed their vows at First United Methodist Church. Bob Anderson stood with Dad as his best man, Marc Yates walked my mom down the aisle, and my sisters and I stood with her as bridesmaids. Mom wore a rose-pink dress, while Les wore teal, I wore purple, and Lisa wore a dress with tiny rose pink, teal, and purple flowers that tied all of the colors together.

After the ceremony, we had dinner in the banquet room at Albert's, a local restaurant, with approximately fifty people in attendance. Several friends and family members stood to toast my parents, and at some point during the evening, I joined them. I stood behind Mom and Dad, raised my glass, and told them how great they looked and how much I loved them. Though he was walking with a cane by then, Dad looked healthy and happy and seemed to thoroughly enjoy the evening.

* * *

In the months following Dad's return, I learned bits and pieces of the undercover work he had done, partly from my dad and partly from the public praise that poured in. Starting soon after Dad's diagnosis, he received many letters expressing concern for his health and appreciation for his part in bringing down the Mafia in Lodi. Some of these letters came from distinguished public figures: FBI agents he had worked with; attorney Craig Star of the US Department of Justice; Jerry Brown, governor of California; and even President Ronald Reagan.

On October 1, 1980, my parents visited the FBI headquarters in Washington DC, where they met William Webster, then the director of the FBI, who personally presented Dad with a plaque that reads: "To Louis E. Peters, who set new standards of patriotism, of selflessness, and of valor, with the gratitude and respect of his FBI friends." Webster also appointed Dad an honorary FBI agent, bringing him a step closer to his childhood dream.

On the same trip back east, my parents stopped in New York so Dad could be interviewed by David Hartman for an episode of *Good Morning America*. From there, the "Lou Peters story" appeared in *Reader's Digest*, *People* magazine, *Newsweek*, and newspapers across the country.

In fall of 1980, a fifth-grade class at Live Oak School in Milford, Connecticut, read about my dad's heroism in one of these articles. The students were so impressed by Dad's unselfish patriotism that they each wrote a letter to him and shared their personal thoughts on what he had done. Dad wrote back to the students and sent each of them a T-shirt with the car dealership logo, promising to visit if he was ever in Milford.

True to his word, in April 1981, Dad contacted the students' teacher, Bill Corkery, when he made a trip back east to see his uncles. Though Dad now walked cautiously with a cane and wore tinted glasses because his eyesight was failing, he still made time to meet his twenty-three pen pals and answer questions about his work as an FBI informant and his brain tumor.

One of the students asked Dad what alias he was known by when undercover. "My own," he replied. "You have two things that are very precious and valuable, which only you can build or destroy: your name and your reputation."

When another student asked how much Dad got paid, he said, "Nothing. The FBI wanted to pay me, but I said no, you don't have enough money to give me to do this for money, so I'll do it for free. There comes a time when you have to stand up for what's right."[3]

Dad was so proud of his achievement and of setting an example of what it means to be a patriot and do what's right. He wanted to write a book about his work as a "concerned citizen" and started recording thoughts on his childhood, tour in Korea, college degrees, and early jobs with General Motors. He even decided on a title—*Honor Thy Country*, intended to be a retort to Gay Talese's book on Joe Bonanno Sr., *Honor Thy Father*.

To keep all of the newspaper articles in one place, Dad asked me to help him fill several 20×25-inch scrapbooks that held full newspaper pages. I was a bit hesitant, not because I didn't want to help him, but because I didn't want to look at the newspapers. From the day six years earlier when I heard the *Lodi News Sentinel* was going to print a story about the Second Coming, I

---

3 Details taken from an article by Carolyn Milazzo: "Live Oaks Kids Meet Pen Pal; Genuine Hero Pays a Visit," The Milford Citizen, April 15, 1981, p. 3.

never looked at or even touched a newspaper. In our house, the newspaper usually sat on or near the kitchen table. Whenever I walked in, I would glance at the table. If the newspaper was there, I would quickly avert my eyes. I was terrified of seeing a headline announcing my impending death.

For Dad, however, I faced my fear. As I read the articles and realized the magnitude of what my hero had accomplished, part of me felt like I had been saved forever, that there was no way God would come back to earth during my lifetime. I just knew Dad's sacrifice and patriotism would be talked about for years to come.

Then I snapped back to reality and remembered that God had already cut my dad's life short, turning my permanent safety into absolute uncertainty.

* * *

In early January 1981, it became clear the normal course of radiation wasn't working. We had one last option: Dad qualified for an experimental study being conducted at the University of California, San Francisco, Medical Center.

My sisters and I traveled with my parents to UCSF, where the doctors implanted radioactive "seeds" into Dad's brain and then moved him to a special room. Once my dad was settled, we put on protective clothing and then entered an adjacent room and talked to him through an intercom behind a thick pane of glass. Dad stayed there for three days, after which the implants were removed and he returned home.

Two months after returning from UCSF Medical Center, Dad was interviewed by Roger Young, FBI inspector in charge of public affairs, about his involvement in taking down Joe Bonanno Sr. Without any formal training, my dad had been able to win the Old Man's trust and secure evidence that led to a conviction—something no agent had been able to do. The FBI wanted to use this video and Dad's experience as a tool in training new recruits to achieve similar convictions, specifically related to the Mafia in the United States.[4]

Dad received one more honor for his work with the FBI. In 1972, the Bureau started recognizing private citizens who go above and beyond to help in FBI investigations. This Meritorious Private Service Award is the highest honor the Justice Department bestows on private citizens, and on June 12, 1981, Dad became the fifth person in history to receive it.

Our whole family attended the ceremony in Sacramento. When Robert Young presented the award, he stated, "The FBI had worked more than thirty years to catch Bonanno but couldn't do it until Lou came along. He has worked for the FBI in a capacity few could say they have served."

By then, Dad was in a wheelchair, not able to walk on his own. When he received the award, however, he said, "I'm not supposed to get up, but I'm going to anyway." My mom helped him stand, and he delivered the first few minutes of his speech on his feet,

---

4   This interview is available online: "The Lou Peters Story," FBI.gov, no date, https://www.fbi.gov/video-repository/newss-the-lou-peters-story/view

speaking with difficulty. Then he became unsteady, so Mom helped him back into his chair, and he continued his speech from there. Dad thanked the FBI for the support he received and said that even though he gave up his last healthy years for the FBI, he would do it all again.

It was such a bittersweet moment. Dad looked so proud in his three-piece suit, receiving a tremendous honor, yet his time was limited. The audience was gracious and waited patiently for him to finish his speech, but I saw their pitying, knowing looks. Since my sisters and I were up front, in clear view of those present, I made sure they saw my look of unwavering pride and love for my dad.

At the end of June, Dad returned to San Francisco for follow-up scans, which revealed that the experimental treatment hadn't worked. Nothing else could be done. From that point on, Dad spent his time napping, visiting with friends, and working on his story.

One day, two brothers from a family we had known for years visited Dad and talked to him about God. I stayed in the next room, straining to hear what they were saying. I heard words like "God" and "soul," so I assumed they were talking to him about getting "saved" and going to heaven. *No, no, no! Dad, don't listen to that,* I thought. *You can't believe that. Please don't go to the other side, don't go to the other side.* I started to panic at the thought of my dad choosing God.

Finally, I couldn't take it anymore and walked into the living room. "Hi, Dad. What are you guys doing?"

Hi honey, we're having a private conversation. It's okay, why don't you go back into the family room."

"Okay, Dad," I replied and walked back into the family room, terrified. At one point, I heard them praying together. My dad didn't go to church or read the Bible, so I knew he was praying to find peace, not knowing what would happen to him after he died, but still—I didn't want him to choose God when that was the opposite of what I was likely going to do.

I never asked my dad about any part of that conversation, for the same reason I couldn't tell him about my conversation with Lori and Debbie seven years earlier when I called him into my room. I was too afraid to hear him say he believed it.

Though Dad didn't seem scared of dying, he didn't want to be alone when he left this earth. When he took naps, he often asked me to stay with him until he fell asleep—not unlike my request for him to stay with me when I was thirteen. We would lie on our sides, facing the same direction, his arm draped over my shoulders, and we'd talk and sometimes laugh until he fell asleep.

One day during nap time, Dad asked me a surprising question. "So, what do you do when you and Brian are alone?" he asked out of the blue.

"Oh, well, why do you want to know?" I replied, glad he couldn't see my face turning red.

"Well...you know, when you guys are alone...maybe you want to talk to your Mom about protection."

"Oh, it's okay. I've already talked with Mom, and everything is taken care of."

"Okay, good. I'm glad you talked with your mom."

Of course, Mom never talked to me about protection—I got that information from a free clinic Debbie and I went to years earlier—but his concern was so sweet. I loved him for it and wanted to put his mind at ease.

In mid-July 1981, Dad developed pneumonia and went back into the hospital. The doctor told Mom these would be his final days. In the early afternoon of July 18, my mom took me to see Dad. Lying there unconscious, he looked so old and weak, a shell of the man he once was. During those final days, I stayed by his side, night and day. How could I leave? My person, my hero, was dying.

That first night when visiting hours were coming to an end, my mom offered to take me home. "You can come back tomorrow."

"I am not leaving Dad alone," I said emphatically. "You can go home, Mom. I'll be fine."

She decided to stay. Mom slept in a large chair in the corner of the room, and I grabbed three armless wood chairs, pushed them together, and created my sleeping quarters for the next two nights. I spent most of the time holding Dad's hand and talking to him. "Please keep breathing. Please wake up. I love you so much."

On the third day, Bob Anderson came to visit. As Mom, Bob, and I talked and laughed about Dad's FBI experience and some of his "stunts," he started making loud gasping sounds. I jumped up and ran to the nurse's station and said, "Hurry! My Dad's waking up. Hurry! Hurry!" Then I rushed back to the room.

The nurse followed shortly after and walked straight to Dad's bedside. As she checked Dad's heart and pulse, she explained, "Those noises were the final spontaneous sounds a body makes."

"But, I heard him trying to wake up," I said.

"No, I'm sorry. Your dad is gone."

At the very moment the nurse was checking on Dad, my sister Les called the room. My mom answered and told her, "Dad just now passed away." Bob Anderson expressed his sympathies to Mom and me and then left.

I sat down in one of the wooden chairs, feeling shocked and defeated. Through my tears, I watched Dad turn to the color of death.

"I love you, Dad," I whispered.

Mom leaned over Dad and hugged him, shedding tears in front of me for the first time. I had never seen her so vulnerable.

About ten minutes later, three orderlies walked in and started preparing Dad to be moved from his bed to the gurney.

"Where are you taking him?" I asked as I jumped up. "I want to come with my dad."

"I'm sorry, but you can't come with us," one of them said.

"What do you mean I can't? I want to be with him!"

They covered Dad with a sheet and wheeled him past me. I felt sick, imagining what my dad's body would be enduring, and began to cry harder. I sat down on the hard wooden chair and shook uncontrollably. I bent forward in the chair, elbows on my knees and head in my hands, rocking forward and back, forward and back.

After the orderlies left, the nurse asked if I wanted something to calm myself.

"No, I don't want anything," I told her.

Mom spoke up. "Lori, why don't you have something."

"No, mom, I don't want anything!"

I wanted to—I needed to—feel what I was feeling. My dad was worth every ounce of sadness and sorrow I was experiencing. I didn't give a shit what I looked like or sounded like.

Looking back, I believe my dad chose that moment to let go. He knew Lisa wasn't there and felt this was a way to protect her from the raw shock. He knew Les was calling the room. He knew Bob, Mom, and I were talking about his exploits. He knew it was time.

After Dad died, there were rumors that his death had been staged by the FBI for his protection, or that he had been murdered by a Mafia hit. Neither of those was true. I was there. I watched him die.

After Dad's death, the FBI, in conjunction with the Society of Former Special Agents of the FBI, renamed the Meritorious Private Service Award that he had received just a month earlier. The following year, they started presenting the Louis E. Peters Memorial Service Award to private citizens who selflessly give their time and service to help the FBI, an award that is still presented to this day.

* * *

My dad died on July 20, 1981, a little more than a year from the time he was given six months to live. We held his memorial and graveside services four days later.

Before Dad's funeral, Mom took my sisters and me clothes shopping because she wanted us to look cohesive and appropriate for the day. The last thing on my mind was what I would wear, but I knew appearances were important to Mom, so I went along to appease her.

When we arrived at the church on the day of the funeral, we were led into a separate room to wait for the service to start. Dad's open coffin sat in an adjacent viewing room for immediate and extended family only. My younger sister Lisa wanted to go see Dad. When he entered the hospital with pneumonia, Lisa had been on a twenty-eight-day high-school-sponsored international tour and arrived home two days after he died. She never got to say goodbye and wanted that closure. I walked with Lisa to the viewing room and hung back while she approached the coffin.

Just before the service began, we took our seat in the front pew, across from the Marine color guard. I recall that I quietly cried as Dad was remembered, but other than that, the service is a blank.

From the church, we were driven to the gravesite, where some people filled in the rows of chairs that sat under a large cloth awning, while others milled around chatting. It was a beautiful sunny day, a day Dad would have loved because of sunshine, the Marines, the FBI, and his family and friends all together.

The chairs faced Dad's coffin, which was raised above his soon-to-be forever spot on earth. *I don't want Dad in the ground*, I thought when I saw the coffin. *I wish he was at sea.* He loved the water—swimming, boating, and sunning himself near our pool or by the ocean—and dreamed of owning a yacht one day. Dad once told me that if he had known about the Navy when he was young, he would have enlisted.

"Why?" I asked.

"Then I would have been on the water."

Dad received a hero's burial with all the trimmings: police motor-cade, Marine color guard, twenty-one-gun salute, flag-draped coffin, FBI special agents, and the Lodi chief of police as pall-bearers. I believe one of the Marines handed the folded flag to my mom, but it was difficult to see from where I was sitting, which was not up front with my mom and sisters where I should have been. When I walked up to sit with them, I found that the front row had been taken by other relatives. Next to my mom was her brother,

Bob, then Les, then my dad's brother, Paul, and then Lisa. Paul held both of my sisters' hands, while I was left to sit in another row by myself. I felt so insignificant. Partway through the ceremony, my dad's office manager, Jackie, walked up behind me and put her hands on my shoulders. I will never forget her kindness, knowing how I must have felt sitting alone at my father's burial.

After the service, we were driven home. In no time at all, people showed up with their food and their *I'm so sorrys*. I wanted to vomit. To escape their pitying looks, well-meaning words, and prayers, I grabbed Dad's favorite shoes—the comfortable Birkenstocks he started wearing during treatment—and walked out the front door. I stood on the lawn, clutching his shoes to my chest, just wanting the world to stop. *Stop, time, stop. Please. Everyone is going to forget Dad. He has to be remembered. This just can't be happening!*

I started to panic. It didn't help that it was bright and sunny out. But I couldn't go back inside with all those well-wishers. *Fuck off,* I wanted to tell them. *My dad is dead. He's gone and will be forgotten.* I felt so raw and lonely and anxious, and I didn't know how I was going to survive.

Right there on the front lawn, clinging to his Birkenstocks, I made him a promise: "Dad, I will finish the book you started. I don't know when and I don't know how, but the world will not forget you. They will know you like I know you—as the hero you are."

Me

After my dad died, I felt lost. My fears increased, and I started having panic attacks inside the house as well as outside, since it became clear that my home, my fortress, was now penetrable. God was still stalking me, and now my protector was gone.

To escape, I started binge eating, especially sweets, and after my mom commented on my increasing weight, I began purging. I stopped seeing Brian, and when I wasn't coping with bulimia, I was having sex with guys I barely knew.

I tried to distract myself with work too, but I didn't have a passion for any particular career path. Back when I learned that God could appear any minute, I stopped dreaming about what I wanted to be someday. I didn't think I'd be alive to pursue it, so what was the point? I had been working as a dental assistant when my dad died, but that didn't last long. The work itself helped me focus because it was up close in an enclosed space, but I didn't really care about the job and soon quit.

This pattern of starting and stopping careers repeated itself over the next several years. I became a hairstylist, massage therapist, life insurance salesperson, EKG technician, and flight attendant, but none of them were my dream. It was hard enough to get to work and stay focused, so once I lost interest, I quit and moved on. The only thing I really cared about was telling my Dad's story, but at that point, I was in no shape to take on such a huge project.

By 1982, I was engaged to John, a guy I didn't know too well. We were living together in an apartment in Lodi, and I was working at another meaningless job, this time in manufactured home sales.

One weekend, I accompanied my manager, Bill, and another saleswoman, Barbara, to a mobile home show event at a large convention center in Sacramento. On the last night, after showing and selling our three lines of homes, the three of us walked across the expansive parking lot toward Bill's car. As we entered a breezeway, I noticed a frail, hunched, dark-skinned woman walking slowly ahead of us. With one hand, she clutched a long scarf that covered her hair, and with the other hand, she clutched her purse to her chest. I slowed to talk with her and let Bill and Barbara go ahead.

"Hi. Are you here by yourself?" I asked the seemingly elderly woman.

"Yes," she answered, keeping her head down as we walked.

"Do you need a ride? Or is someone picking you up?"

"I do need a ride," she said softly.

"Bill," I called out. "Can we give this woman a ride home?"

Bill turned his head slightly and said, "Sure."

I looked back at the woman and said, "We'd be happy to take you home. Where do you live?"

All of a sudden, this slight, hunched, "elderly" figure stood up to her full height of five foot eleven and started walking briskly in front of me, purposefully swinging the arm that had been folded at her chest, purse in hand. She held the headscarf with her other hand and spoke to herself in a low masculine voice. Then she turned back toward me but didn't really look at me. Instead, she seemed to answer herself in the soft, feminine voice. My mind raced. *Is this woman mentally ill? Is she dangerous? What's in that purse?*

I hurried up to Barbara, who was standing on the passenger's side of the car with the front door open. "We cannot take this person home!" I said frantically, turning my head toward the approaching woman, who was now arguing with herself in two voices. Bill sat in the driver's seat with his door closed. His hearing is bad, so he couldn't hear me, and because he's blind in his left eye, he didn't see the woman approaching the driver's side of the car.

"I am not getting in the car with her!" I said. She was now about a foot away from the back door.

"Lock the doors! Start the car!" Barbara told Bill as she slid into her seat.

"I thought we were taking her home," Bill said, confused.

"No, let's get out of here! Get in, Lori, now!"

I quickly got in and shut the door. As we drove off, I looked back at the woman walking across the dark parking lot, still arguing with herself. I was glad she wasn't sitting next to me in the back-seat, but with the immediate threat gone, I began to wonder what had happened to her. Was she all alone in this world? I couldn't help but feel empathy for people who were different, like me.

I was still shell-shocked when I reached my apartment, and I immediately told my fiancé about the incident.

"Well, things like that are happening in the world," John said. "People are behaving more strangely. I think it's a sign of the end of the world and the Second Coming."

No, this can't be happening! My fiancé believes in the Second Coming? I thought, panic rising. John and I had never talked about religion, and I hadn't mentioned what happened to me.

After that, any time John saw a sign that the world was ending, he told me about it. For my own sanity, I knew I had to get away from him, but I also didn't want to hurt this otherwise sweet guy, so I kept trying to make it work.

For the next few months, I was constantly on edge, constantly anxious because I didn't know when he would make another Second Coming comment. Finally, I couldn't take it anymore, and I broke off the engagement, claiming simply that I didn't think it was going to work between us. I moved back home, quit selling manufactured homes, and tried to figure out my next steps.

* * *

In 1984, while I was going to beauty school for cosmetology and living at home, I met a firefighter named Dan. He was a big guy, handsome and strong, and I was immediately drawn to him. I was so glad the feeling was mutual.

After we started dating, I asked him the question I should have asked John. I really liked Dan, and I had to know his answer before we went any further. So, while driving in his 4-Runner one day, my right hand clutching the passenger armrest so tightly my fingers turning white, I asked, "Are you religious?"

"No, I don't believe in all that. I'm more spiritual," he replied, and I relaxed my grip. *Wow*, I thought. *I think I'm going to stick with this guy!* That hunch was confirmed after I shared details about my sexual past that I had never told anyone. In response, Dan simply said, "We all have pasts, and I really like being with you."

After that, I knew I would never leave him. I had found a one-of-a-kind guy who wasn't religious and accepted me as I was.

At dusk on September 1, 1985, Dan and I exchanged vows in front of a judge on the steps of Lodi's city hall. I was painfully aware that my dad wouldn't be there to walk me down the aisle, so I chose not to have any of the usual wedding traditions. We married in a simple, private ceremony without any guests; our chauffeur and his wife stood in as our witnesses.

From there, we were taken to our outdoor reception at the Wine and Roses Inn, where we were joined by sixty to seventy guests. Betty and Bob from our old Cupertino neighborhood attended, as did Debbie, Lori, and their husbands.

My marriage and reception marked a huge milestone for me. Many times over the preceding years, I had wondered if I would ever find someone like Dan, someone who loved and accepted me in spite of my anxiety issues. I think my family may have wondered the same thing. That night, I felt like I had come a long way in spite of all that had happened. I was happy to be alive to get married, something I didn't think would happen after my conversation with Lori and Debbie, and I was happy they were there to witness it.

Dan and I honeymooned on the foggy Northern California coast in a beautiful honeymoon suite. We were supposed to go horseback riding one day, but I developed a migraine, and we headed back to the room so I could rest. Dan couldn't have been more considerate. He made me feel safe and loved in a way I hadn't felt since my dad had been alive.

* * *

During my senior year of high school, I started working out more consistently, partly because I liked the feeling of being strong and partly because it provided a much-needed distraction. Then, after Dad died, I realized I needed to prioritize working out again to stop the bulimia cycle. I began running the obstacle course with exercise stations at one of the local parks, jogged around the school track, and did pull-ups to work on my arms. When the first gym opened in Lodi—a women's only gym—I joined immediately. I spent so much time working out that the owner hired me to help other women. By the time I met Dan, more gyms had opened in Lodi, and we joined one together and became workout partners.

Before he was famous, John Claude van Damme visited our gym with his bodybuilder girlfriend, who was giving a talk on how she trains and competes. I already had a longstanding interest in the sport, ever since our family went to Palm Springs in 1971 and I saw Arnold Schwarzenegger and a couple other bodybuilders give a posing exhibition. I was in awe. I had never seen anything like it and wanted to marry one of those strong, muscled men someday. Years later, I bought a few women's bodybuilding magazines and occasionally thought, *You know, I think I could do that.* Since Dan had also thought of competing, we decided to turn the possibility into a reality and entered the 1986 Bay Area Bodybuilding Championship.

Talk about hard work! Between the physical strain and strict dieting involved in building muscle, I wanted to quit more than once.

"You can quit," Dan would tell me over a snack of defrosted spinach and vinegar. "Or you can tough it out."

"Shit," I would say, knowing he was right, and show up for leg day the next morning.

Despite the pain of training, or perhaps because of it, my panic attacks were manageable during the months leading up to our competition. I focused on proper diet, lifting, practicing my routine, and perfecting my spray tan. I worked out a lot of anxiety and enjoyed watching my muscles gain definition and strength.

Before the competition, I asked Mom to come to the house so I could show her my routine. She was impressed by my flexibility and all the work I had put in, but bodybuilding wasn't her thing, and she didn't come to the actual competition. When I entered the Mrs. California beauty pageant, however, she attended because it was a *beauty* pageant, not muscle-bound women strutting around.

In the women's division, the participants were placed in one of three categories: lightweight, middleweight, or heavyweight. I hoped for the middleweight group, since it seemed to have fewer competitors, and I made it by one pound.

The day of the competition, I was excited and nervous, but I performed my routine to "Who's That Girl" by the Eurythmics without a mistake. In the end, I didn't win, but I did finish in the top two—out of two participants. Dan entered the highly competitive heavyweight division and won. Afterward, we celebrated with his family—and man, did we eat!

With the bodybuilding competition behind us, Dan and I returned to normal workout and eating habits and a relatively stable life. For many people, this might be a good thing; for me, it was not. I needed excitement and events to help me keep my mind occupied. So, in addition to the bodybuilding contest and Mrs. California beauty pageant representing Lodi, I competed in the Fleet Feet mini triathlon and Lodi Fun Run.

Soon, however, I got tired of creating excitement. Our life became almost boring and left me with too much time to think—and thus, panic. Dan knew I battled with anxiety; he had gone with me to the general practitioner who diagnosed me with generalized anxiety with panic attacks and prescribed anti-anxiety medication. But he didn't know about the incident when I was thirteen and didn't know about the episodes where the world took on an unreal feeling.

I slowly slipped backward. I stopped going to work and struggled to be the wife Dan wanted me to be. The truth is, I didn't know how to be in a relationship or a marriage, for that matter. I didn't know how to take care of a home, cook, or be a partner. It all felt overwhelming. In my effort to not think about God and dying, I had focused on how to be there for someone sexually, but that was it.

Now I felt stuck, scared that I would lose Dan, but not knowing how to "do marriage" so he would want to stay.

* * *

On January 17, 1989, Dan's station house responded to an intense car fire in front of an elementary school in Stockton. After they finally put out the fire, which had been fueled by accelerants stashed in the car, Dan caught sight of someone in camouflage running across the school grounds. As he walked onto the black-top playground to look around, he saw what looked like piles of clothes lying on the ground. When he got closer, he realized the clothes were actually three dead children, shot by Patrick Purdy, the man in camouflage.

By that time, police had located Purdy, who had shot and killed himself. After the police deemed the area safe, Dan and his fellow firefighters entered the building and found a horrific scene: blood-splattered walls and floors, two more dead children lying in the hallway, and many injured kids crouching under desks and tables. In the end, Purdy killed five children and injured twenty-nine more; he also wounded one teacher.

At first, Dan seemed to be fine despite the horrific scene he witnessed. A couple months afterward, we traveled to the FBI Headquarters in Washington DC after I learned that my dad was part of a new permanent Organized Crime exhibit. Right in the center of the display was a photo of Dad, with the story of what he did and a photo of Joe Bonanno Sr. to the side. The tour guide explained the exhibit and then answered some questions. When he finished, I raised my hand and said, "I don't have a question, but I wanted to say that's my father up there." Everyone turned to face me with wide-eyed expressions. I quickly realized what they were thinking. "Oh, I'm Lou Peters's daughter, not Bonanno's!"

Relieved, people approached Dan and I to ask questions and share their amazement at what my dad had accomplished. After the tour guide told his manager I was Lou Peters's daughter, the manager gave Dan and I a special tour of the FBI building, let us fire weapons at paper targets, and sent us home with souvenirs, including the targets and photos taken while holding the guns. We were treated like royalty. Dad would have been proud of the display and of how they treated us. I felt so proud to be his daughter.

In months after our return, Dan started to show signs that the Purdy incident had affected him deeply. He developed PTSD and had difficulty sleeping. He also became distant and short-tempered, and like me, he used sex with strangers to cope with his symptoms.

Dan confessed what he was doing, and I told him I understood, because I had spent many years using the same escape routes for my panic. But my understanding wasn't enough. Ultimately, Dan decided he didn't want to be married anymore. He didn't feel the same about anything in his life, including me.

While part of me could relate, I was terrified at the thought of losing him. Like my dad for so many years, Dan had become my safety net. He was a bodybuilder, a firefighter, a hero. In that sense, he was the closest thing to my dad I had for protection, and I would have done anything to keep our relationship going.

I tried to change Dan's mind, but it didn't work. He started dating someone younger, and I plummeted into a dark place. My panic attacks increased. My mom had remarried, and I didn't see much of her, my dad was gone, and now my marriage was over. I felt alone and empty.

In this state, I met a guy who latched on to the fact that I was going through a divorce and pursued me aggressively. We started dating, and I moved in with him shortly thereafter. After moving in, Rick revealed himself to be emotionally and sometimes physically abusive, like the time he shoved me up against a wall with his hand at my throat and yelled in my face because I bought the wrong chocolate chips, or the time he dragged me off the couch by my hair.

Part of me felt like I deserved this treatment. Part of me wondered how I didn't see it coming. Part of me wondered why I stayed. Rick was a six-foot-five former stunt man, and I was initially drawn to his muscular build—another strong guy who could keep me safe. Only, he did the exact opposite, and he enjoyed the fear he caused in me. After a while, I knew I needed to leave. I was able to think clearly enough to tell myself, *Lori, you deserve more than this. This is not going to be your life. This is not right, and you need to get out of here.*

The first time I tried to leave Rick, I went to my sister Lisa's house, but I finally gave in to his phone calls, apologies, and excuses and went back to him. The next time I gave myself some leverage and took his stash of marijuana, thinking I would blackmail him into letting me leave with the promise that I would tell him where I hid it after he agreed. Instead, he held a gun to my head and demanded that I reveal my hiding place.

After living with Rick for about six months, I left for the last time with help from my sister Les. I got my own place, but that didn't last long. When my divorce was finalized, my anxiety and panic attacks intensified. It got so bad that I called my mom, crying, and told her, "I don't want to live anymore, but I don't want to die either. Mom, I don't know what to do. I'm so scared. I don't want to be here. I don't want to be in this world anymore, and I don't want to die! Mom, what do I do?"

"I will get you help," my mom said. "There are places that can help you. Let me find something for you."

"Ok. Thanks for helping me. I just don't know what else to do."

My mom found a facility in Sacramento, and they admitted me as soon as I told them I had suicidal thoughts. At the time, I was taking Klonopin, an antidepressant to help with my anxiety and panic attacks. It's a highly addictive drug, one that should be stopped slowly under a doctor's care. When they admitted me to the facility, however, they stopped it cold turkey because I was a suicide threat. The withdrawal symptoms sent me into absolute panic. I couldn't sleep. I couldn't function. I sat on my bed, shaking, unable to leave my room because everything felt unreal. One night, I struggled to walk down the hall to a nurses' station and convinced night staff that I needed help, so they put a patch on my arm to lessen the withdrawal symptoms.

For six weeks, I pretended I was fine. Though the withdrawals subsided, my panic attacks and unreal world episodes did not. I did everything required of me—the exercises and programs and activities—just so I could get the hell out of there.

When I left the facility, I moved in with my mom and stepdad for about a year. I took a job selling life insurance and got back on medication, but my panic and anxiety episodes amped up again because

I had too much idle time in the large office area. I quit that job and went to massage therapy school, thinking I could help others relax and while giving myself an opportunity to focus on something up close. As it turned out, I was a natural using the right techniques and pressure for each customer. After having a few male clients expect more than the traditional relaxation massage, I moved to Coeur d' Alene, Idaho, on a whim and opened a small massage studio for chair massage *only*, since customers are not as inclined to want more when fully dressed. I had finally found a place to live sight unseen and began a new chapter of my life.

* * *

Though I didn't think psychologists could help me with my real problem—the imminent Second Coming—I kept trying. I wanted to see if someone could share new strategies to help me deal with my panic attacks.

When I was seventeen or eighteen, I met with one doctor a few times, and then he asked my mother to join us for a session, probably because he (correctly) thought there was more going on and that my mom would provide answers. I knew otherwise.

Oh, this is going to be good, I thought. *He has met his match.*

Within the first few minutes, my mom told the psychologist, "I'm not going to be talking about myself."

"Well, we're not going to be able to help Lori, then," he replied. "If you won't let me ask you questions and get your input, we won't be able to get Lori the help she needs."

"No, I'm not going to be talking about myself. I won't be doing that."

So, that was the end of the session.

I saw that doctor a few more times and told him about my panic attacks and my fear of dying, but nothing about God or what had happened with Lori and Debbie. Then one day, I asked him what he believes happens when we die.

"I think it's just over," he said. "When we die, that's just it."

Though I was terrorized by what Lori and Debbie had shared, I was equally scared by the psychologist's words. I couldn't wrap my head around the fact that death was that final—that when we die, our life simply ends. My curious mind kept trying to put myself in the reality of being dead: the earth would keep spinning, and I would never know what happened here or in heaven. I would simply be gone.

I didn't see that doctor again, and I never asked another psychologist what they thought about death. I knew if I did, I might completely destroy my brain.

After working in massage therapy, I needed a change and ended up becoming a flight attendant. Being enclosed in an airplane and focusing on passengers was the best career. After working several years for Horizon and Continental Airlines, I went to work for United Airlines so I could be based back on the West Coast.

Twenty years after asking the doctor about his view of death, I was living in a suburb of Seattle, Washington, working as a flight attendant for United Airlines, my third and final airline. I decided to seek a psychologist's help once again, this time from a doctor referred by a therapist I had been seeing in California.

On my first meeting with every other doctor, they would say, "Come on in and take a seat," and I would wonder if the seat I chose was the one they wanted me to choose. With Dr. Peterson, I deliberately chose a chair I didn't think he wanted me to sit in, the one closest to his desk. When he walked in, he immediately asked, "Why did you choose that chair?"

"I was just wondering if you would notice or care," I said.

"So, you were testing me."

"Yep."

"No one has ever tried to test me," he replied and smiled. That interaction set me at ease from the beginning. We simply clicked, and within a session or two, I felt comfortable enough to tell him most of the story, not just my anxiety and panic attacks, but my conversation with Lori and Debbie about the Second Coming, too. I left out the episodes where the world seemed fake, because I wasn't sure how to explain them.

After I finished, I waited, wondering if he would think I was crazy or confirm that God was coming, or both.

He did neither, and his response changed everything.

"Lori, what happened to you was very traumatic," he said. "It caused PTSD, which developed into panic attacks and anxiety when you didn't receive the help you needed."

I sat there, stunned. Ever since I felt my brain shift twenty-five years earlier, I thought something was physically wrong. I never connected the brain shift with my fear, anxiety, and panic attacks, or thought they might all have one legitimate cause.

"How could I have PTSD from that conversation?" I asked.

"You grew up feeling like your parents were keeping information from you. That, along with your curious personality and both of your best friends confirming that God is coming to take everyone, created a perfect storm for PTSD. Having only one friend telling you about God is not as powerful as having both friends confirming it."

I felt a combination of relief and sadness—relief that my brain wasn't broken and sadness for the life I never had because I was too terrified to reveal my secret.

* * *

In the twenty-two years since that conversation with Dr. Peterson, I have learned to manage my anxiety. Now that I understand what happened and why I reacted as I did, I am able to cope on my own. I stopped relying on big, strong men to protect me, and I created my own "fortress"—a home that I share with two cats and my canine coworker; a home that I have decorated and updated according to my tastes, not to please anyone else; a home where I feel safe and secure.

I have also researched PTSD and learned that one form, called Complex PTSD, usually happens to children or adolescents who live in a war zone or experience physical abuse or some other condition that persists for years and carries the constant threat of death. This kind of PTSD often includes dissociative disorders, one of which is derealization.

The first time I read the description of derealization, I cried. It perfectly captured what I had been experiencing for forty-seven years: episodes of living in a fog, feeling disconnected from the world around me, seeing the world as a fake, two-dimensional movie set. As a teenager and adult, I knew I was suffering from more than anxiety and panic attacks, but I couldn't tell anyone about the derealization experience because I didn't have the words to describe it.

Though I still experience two-dimensional episodes, I can now quickly turn my head or otherwise refocus my attention and break the sense of nonreality. I still have two panic attack triggers—long drives or walks on sunny days in flat, expansive areas and thinking about the meaning of life and what will happen after I die. The external triggers are easier to avoid, but in general, my panic attacks no longer take over and render me helpless.

For the last eighteen years, I have owned and operated a barbershop named Snip n Sail—Snip as a tribute to my sister Les, who would say, "Let me snip your hair" whenever I wanted a change, and Sail as a tribute to my dad and his love of the water, a perfect fit since my shop happens to be at a marina. Thanks to Dad, I learned how to run a business and treat people so that they become long-time customers.

After my dad died, my mom remarried and created a new life for herself with her husband and stepchildren. We stayed in touch, but we always lacked the connection I had hoped to have.

In her later years, my mom was diagnosed with Alzheimer's disease, which progressed to the point where she needed full-time care. By that time, her second husband had been diagnosed with Parkinson's and could no longer care for Mom, and Lisa was teaching full time, so we decided to move Mom close to me, since my job offered more flexibility.

One of my barbershop customers volunteers his time and jet for Angel Flight West, a nonprofit that offers free flights for veterans needing to be transported for medical care. In August 2016, Jeff flew me to Sacramento to pick up my mom and bring her back to a care facility in Washington State.

After mom was settled, I started closing my barbershop an hour early so I could be with her every day for dinnertime at the facility. Mom still remembered me and introduced me to the other patients. Each day when it came time to leave, I would walk a few steps away from her table and then turn back and wave. She would wave back and smile. Then I would turn around and walk a few more steps away, turn back and wave. She would return my wave and smile. I continued this routine all the way to the security door, and just before I stepped out, Mom would give me a big smile and a wave that said, "Okay, enough already."

I will always treasure the smiles she gave me during those last few months. They were deep and genuine, expressing the connection I rarely had with her growing up.

In November 2016, Mom had a brain bleed and never regained consciousness. As I had with Dad, I stayed by her side night and day, and on the third day, she made the same gasping noises and then passed away. Despite our differences, I loved my mom, and I'm so grateful I was able to be with her at the very end.

Epilogue

In 1990, Dad was featured in an episode of *Story Behind the Story*, along with segments on John Lennon, Bob Hope, and Apollo 11. He would have been amused that he shared television time with such star power.

As part of this production, a television crew came to my mom and stepdad's home. My mom, my sisters, and I were all filmed separately, and the interviewer asked each of us a different question about my dad's work with the FBI. Though my sisters and I had never done anything like this, we all appeared calm and answered the questions clearly. I felt nervous, but also very proud to talk about my dad.

When it was my turn, the interviewer asked, "What was your dad hoping would come from his undercover work?"

"He felt that if he didn't do it, nobody would," I replied. "If he set an example, then maybe other people would follow if the same thing happened in their town. That was very important to him."

If Dad had seen the episode, he would have criticized the acting, especially that of the person who played him, and rightly so—the actor didn't have anywhere near the personality of my dad. At the same time, Dad would have eaten it up. He would have been excited to see his experience replayed for television viewers.

Now, forty years after I stood on our front lawn, clutching Dad's Birkenstocks, I have kept my promise and finished the book he started.

Dad never knew what I went through, but I have imagined what it would be like for him to read this book and find out. I picture him hugging me tightly as he says, "Honey, I am so proud of you and all you have accomplished. I understand why you waited to keep your promise, and I am so sorry for what you went through."

"Dad, you gave me everything I needed to not give up. I had your love, humor, focus, and drive to keep me going and tell your story. Dad, you saved me."

Then he would make me laugh by sharing more pranks he pulled on Bob Anderson, and we would reminisce about Dad's MacGyver moves and the years we shared together.

"Dad, what happens when we die?"

"Lori, honey, I wish I could tell you, but death is unexplainable. What I can tell you is, in your final moments, if you feel afraid, remember how much I love you and how incredibly proud I am that you are my daughter."

"I promise."

Dad working the farm in Carmel, Maine, with his team of horses, 1946

Dad with his mom, dad, and brother Paul, 1947

Dad on a naval ship heading home from Korea, 1953

Dad receiving his master's degree from Michigan State University with Mom, 1958

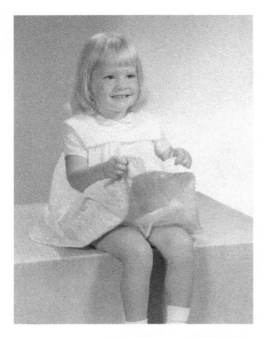

First photo shoot, 1963

Dad, me, and Les with Cinnamon on our parents' bed, Dearborn, Michigan, 1965

Family photo, 1966. Left to right: Dad, Les, mom, me. Lisa in Mom's lap

Mom and Dad at a General Motors black-tie event in San Francisco, 1968

*My family's home in
Lodi, 1970-1981*

Dad loving the sun by a pool, 1971

Sixth grade was my best school year, when I won the math contest and realized there was so much more to discover than boys. Left to right: Mr. Chappell on the far left; me, top row center; Lori, next to me; Principal Dillon on the far right. Tim is directly in front of me.

Mom and Dad coming back with a catch after a chartered fishing trip, Florida, 1971

Sacramento harness horse races, 1972. Dad's dealership's sponsored horse came in third place. Left to right: the horse's owner/trainer, the driver, me, and the owner's son.

Celebrating my twelfth birthday, November 1972. Left to right: Lori, Dad, me

A family photo around Dad's beloved broken brown leather recliner, 1975. Back row, left to right: Me, Dad, Les. Seat, left to right: Mom, Grammy Peters.

Me working the reception desk at Dad's dealership, 1976

Joe Bonanno gave my dad a signed framed copy of the Parade cover story dated February 12, 1978: "To Dear Friend Lou, with affection. J. Bonanno."

FBI surveillance photo, 1978. Left to right: Dad, Jack DiFilippi, Bill Bonanno

Dad and me after I graduated from Lodi High School, 1978

Dad in his "not standing out" attire, on his way to catch a flight to meet Bob Anderson in San Diego, 1980

Marc Yates (seated) visiting Dad at the safe house in La Jolla, California, 1980

Signed autograph of President Ronald Reagan, 1980

Lisa, Les, and me as
bridesmaids for our mom,
September 1980

Bob Anderson standing
next to my dad, the groom,
September 1980

Giving a toast at the reception after my parents renewed their vows, September 1980

Dad receiving a plaque from FBI director William Webster with Mom standing by, Washington DC, FBI Headquarters, October 1980

The ceremony when Dad received the Meritorious Private Service Award at the Sacramento FBI headquarters, June 12, 1981. Top row, left to right: Bob Anderson; Ray Yelchak, special agent in charge of the Sacramento office; Mom; Roger Young; me; Les. Seated, left to right: Lisa, Dad.

Marc Yates (right), Bob Anderson (third back on the left), and other FBI agents carrying Dad's coffin after his church service, July 20, 1981

Dan and me at our wedding reception, Wine and Roses Inn, Lodi, California, September 1, 1985

Performing my routine at the 1986 Bay Area Bodybuilding Championships

A rehearsal meeting during Mrs. California pageant, Los Angeles, 1987. Left to Right: Mrs. Lancaster and me, Mrs. Lodi

Standing in front of the Organized Crime exhibit featuring Dad, spring 1989

Modeling at age thirty after the divorce filing, 1990

Me and another Horizon Airlines flight attendant, 1996

Deliberation by Mario Sanchez Nevado hangs in my home. This is the most accurate representation of what I truly believed would happen if I asked my dad about the Second Coming and he confirmed it was true.

Acknowledgments

To former Special Agent Robert "Bob" Anderson. When I think of all you did to support and protect my dad, the word *wow* comes to mind. My dad was incredibly lucky to have you in his corner. Thank you for your expertise and concern, and for putting up with Dad's humorous stunts as well as his stubborn streak. You and Dad had an amazing bond. Together, you were an unstoppable force. Thank you for your emails, photos, and conversations, all of which added tremendous value in telling Dad's story. Thank you for your unwavering support and kindness.

To former Special Agent Carl Larsen. Thank you for expertly installing an incredibly elaborate electronic monitoring system and for keeping Dad's Nagra recorder working properly and securely. Thank you for your contribution to this book through conversations, emails, and photos, as well as your kind words and support.

To the FBI personnel and special agents that Dad worked with. Thank you for supporting my dad in a once-in-a-lifetime opportunity to serve his country. He so admired and appreciated the difficult and dangerous work you do.

To the grand jury who decided to indict Joe Bonanno Sr. and Jack DiFilippi. Thank you for your duty and your time.

To the US attorneys and staff involved in the Bonanno-DiFilippi trial. Thank you for preparing my dad to give his testimony.

To the Honorable Judge William Ingram. Thank you for your hard work presiding over the trial and for the words spoken about my dad's contribution to the verdict. He felt so incredibly proud.

To Marc Yates. Thank you for being one of Dad's true friends. I will always remember your friendship and loyalty during some difficult times before the Mafia entered our lives. I wish you were still with us.

To Mr. Chappell, one of the greatest teachers inside and outside of the classroom. Though you are gone, I will never forget what I was able to accomplish in your class, the times you snuck the class out to swim at your member-only city pool and clubhouse, and your personalized addition to my report card, creating a Sense of Humor category every quarter and "grading" me with a +! each time.

To Dr. Peterson. Thank you for your insight and for giving me a safe environment in which to reveal what I had kept bottled up for twenty-five years. My only regret is that I didn't continue my sessions with you to reveal all. I am forever grateful for the precious gift you gave me: explaining "the perfect storm" behind my trauma.

To Vince Streano, the amazing photographer who took my author photograph and reproduced old photos to include in my book. Thank you for your hard work and a fun photo session.

To my family, friends, and my barbershop posse. Thank you for your kind words of encouragement. Your support means so much to me.

To my niece, Tara. Holding you as a newborn meant more than you know. You are the closest I will come to having a child of my own, and I am so proud of you and the young woman you have become: talented, accomplished, and beautiful inside and out. I love you, always.

To Scribe Media. I am so incredibly grateful that your company exists. I'm convinced that having everything I needed to get my book published under one roof was the only way I could see this through. The formula of creating a team for every author's wants and needs from beginning to end is invaluable. I will be forever grateful and your biggest fan—well, if not biggest, close to it.

To my personal Scribe team. Thank you for your incredibly hard work and for putting up with my passion, humor, cussing, tears, and lack of computer skills.

To Rikki Jump, my author strategist. I was so nervous about telling my story along with my dad's, but you put me at ease from our first interview.

To Emily Anderson, my experience coordinator. Thank you for your valuable help and your support to get me started with an incredible team. I actually have a team!

To Katie Orr, my publishing manager. Thank you for keeping me on track and for addressing my questions and concerns.

To Gail Fay, my editor and collaborator. I am finding it difficult to express how grateful I am for you. At first, I wasn't sure if we could work together, having different personalities. I couldn't have been more wrong. We became a great team and balanced each other. You gave me the safety and confidence to reveal all of me without judgment. You provided validation that including my story with Dad's is not only important but necessary. You, Gail, are awesome, and I'm so thankful you came into my life.

Skyler White, my title expert. I'm in awe that you agreed with what I came up with, making just one tiny but important change.

Katherine (Kathy) Shady, my cover designer. Thank you for turning my concept into a wonderful cover.

Cristina Ricci, my copywriter. Thank you for understanding me and for your brilliant choice of words on the back cover.

Girls, we rocked it!

To my team and to everyone behind the scenes at Scribe Media who had a part in the completion of my book. Thank you for helping me keep my promise.

With love, Lori

About the Author

For forty years, Lori Lee Peters has made it her mission to finish her father's story. Now, with *God, the Mafia, My Dad, and Me*, Lori makes her literary debut and confronts the demons of her past—demons that left her with undiagnosed PTSD for years. Lori owns and operates a barbershop in Washington State and shares her home with two cats and her canine co-worker, Leo.

CPSIA information can be obtained
at www.ICGtesting.com
Printed in the USA
BVHW090442111022
649116BV00002B/57

9 781544 525921